Tasty Cute

25 Amigurumi Gourmet Treats

Tasty Cute

25 Amigurumi Gourmet Treats

Annie Obaachan

BARRON'S

A QUANTUM BOOK

First edition for the United States, its territories and
possessions, Canada, and the Philippines published
in 2011 by Barron's Educational Series, Inc.

All inquiries should be addressed to:
Barron's Educational Series, Inc.
250 Wireless Boulevard
Hauppauge, New York 11788
www.barronseduc.com

ISBN-13: 978-0-7641-4727-2

Library of Congress Control Number: 2011927854

This book is published and produced by
Quantum Books
6 Blundell Street
London N7 9BH

QUMTC2A

Printed and bound in Singapore by Star Standard
Industries (Pte) Ltd.

9 8 7 6 5 4 3 2 1

Design: Jeremy Tilston
Photographer: Marcos Bevilacqua
Managing Editor: Julie Brooke
Project Editor: Samantha Warrington
Assistant Editor: Jo Morley
Production Manager: Rohana Yusof
Publisher: Sarah Bloxham

Contents

Cute, Cute, Cute

Welcome to the Wonderful World of Amigurumi

What is amigurumi?

The word *amigurumi* is a combination of the words *ami* and *nuigurumi*. *Ami* means "knit/crochet" in Japanese and *nuigurumi* means "stuffed toy". Put them together, and you have a crocheted stuffed toy.

No one really knows where amigurumi came from. There have always been handmade toys in Japan. Japan has a rich history in textiles, as we can see in weaving for kimonos, the Japanese traditional costume. But there is no such history of knitting or crochet. The Japanese simply took these Western crafts and, instead of using them for purely functional items like socks and scarves, they started to create little animals. Nowadays there are hundreds of amigurumi exhibitions and clubs, not only in Japan but all over the world.

The birth of amigurumi may have been greatly influenced by Japanese traditional doll culture, which has a long history. Hina Matsuri, a doll festival in honor of Girls' Day, is celebrated on the third of March every year, just in time for the peach blossoms. The Odairi-sama/Ohina-sama dolls, representing the Emperor and the Empress, are displayed for this festival by each family with a daughter to ensure her future happiness. This set of dolls tends to be handed down from generation to generation with love, respect, and a sense of history. Boys also have a special doll festival in May.

The dolls stay with Japanese children all their lives, lifting their spirits in times of stress and trouble. Amigurumi animals are an extension of this doll culture, brightening up cloudy days and providing a source of comfort at the toughest of times.

The last few years have witnessed a flowering of Japanese subcultures worldwide. A particularly popular feature of this phenomenon is the Japanese kawaii culture. The closest translation of *kawaii* in English is "cute." From Hello Kitty to Pokémon, anime to manga, cute Japanese characters have swarmed across the world and conquered our hearts. Amigurumi creations also swam with this kawaii-tide. Small, cute, and easy to make, how could they fail to captivate us?

In Japan, people like to keep these animals with them throughout the day. You will see them hanging off bags next to lucky charms, or sitting atop computers and piles of work in the office. Amigurumi characters can comfort and reassure us in this hectic world, secretly saying: "Why don't you take a little break and relax?"

Anyone can master amigurumi, and there are no limits to what you can create. Grab some yarn and crochet hooks, get comfortable by the fire, and start making your own little world.

Tools and Materials

Basic Crochet Kit

Crochet hooks come in a great variety of materials, from wooden and plastic to chunky steel and even ivory. All come in different shapes and sizes. Different countries have different sizing systems — which can be confusing — so always double-check your hook against the conversion charts. Check also that you are using the correct size hook as indicated in the pattern. All of the patterns in this book use a size C crochet hook. However, remember that experimenting with various weights and types of yarn will require different-sized hooks; the important thing is to use a hook that will give a nice tight crochet with the selected yarn.

Knitter's pins with large heads (useful for pinning shapes)

Tapestry needle for sewing up

Split stitch markers for marking the beginnings of rounds.

Tape measure

Sharp scissors

Tweezers to help with stuffing

Embroidery needle for embroidering faces and details.

Embroidery thread

Well-spun yarns are the ideal choice if you want to achieve neat, tidy work.

Fine crochet cotton (lace) thread has a firm texture, that is good for very small details. Its thickness is given in numbers, i.e., 5, 10, and so on. The higher the number, the finer the thread.

4-ply yarn (worsted weight) is good in general, especially for making smaller items.

Double knit (DK) yarn is good for making large pieces, but make sure the crochet is as tight as possible so the stuffing can't be seen. You can achieve different results in amigurumi depending on what size or type of yarn you use, even when you are working on the same pattern. The thicker the yarn, the bigger your amigurumi will be! Just remember to use the right size hook for your yarn — look on the ball band for this information.

Mohair is good for anything you want to have a fluffy texture.

Fancy yarns, such as tweed-effect wools, lurex and bouclé yarns, can be used to create texture and add interesting decorative details.

Cotton wadding and **polyester fiberfill** are the most commonly used materials for stuffing amigurumi, but you could also use scraps of yarn for the really tiny parts.

Small wooden sticks for any parts that need a little support to stay upright.

Techniques

Tasty Cute

Reading Patterns

If this is the first time that you have used crochet patterns, you might feel like you are learning a new language. However, you will soon begin to recognize the abbreviations used in crochet. The abbreviations make patterns shorter and easier to follow.

Let's learn the new crochet language.

Crochet Abbreviations

alt	alternate
approx	approximately
beg	begin/beginning
bet	between
ch	chain stitch
cm	centimeter(s)
col	color
cont	continue
sc	single crochet
sc2tog	single crochet 2 stitches together
tc	triple crochet
dec	decrease/decreases/decreasing
foll	follow/follows/following
hdc	half-double crochet
inc	increase/increases/increasing
mm	millimeter
rep	repeat(s)
sl st	slip stitch
st(s)	stitch(es)
tog	together
dc	double crochet
dc2tog	double crochet 2 stitches together
yo	yarn over hook
*	repeat that step

Now, it's time to step into the hook-sizing world.

Both letters and numbers can appear on the packaging of crochet hooks. The metric sizing is the actual measurement of the hook. The letter is the U.S. sizing range. Lettering may vary, so always rely on the metric sizings.

METRIC	USA
2.5 mm	B
3 mm	C
3.25 mm	D
3.5 mm	E
4 mm	F
4.25 mm	G
5 mm	H
5.5 mm	I
6 mm	J
7 mm	K
8 mm	L
9 mm	M
10 mm	N
15 mm	P

How to read a Japanese crochet chart
On the Japanese chart, each stitch is shown as follows:

- **Magic ring:** tiny circle in the middle of circular chart   O
- **Single crochet:** cross   X
- **Double crochet:** T symbol   Ŧ
- **Chain stitch:** tiny oval   o
- **Increasing:** arrow pointing toward the center of the diagram   >
- **Decreasing:** arrow pointing away from the center of the diagram   <
- **Slip stitch:** black oval   ●

Follow the chart from the center to the outside, then move to the non-circular part of the chart, if there is one shown above the circular part. Always follow the chart counterclockwise.

Crochet Techniques

Crochet is all about mixing really simple techniques with more elaborate flourishes. Once you get the hang of making chains, you are ready to progress to a variety of fancy stitches.

Holding the hook and yarn

Learning how to hold the hook and yarn correctly is the first step to crochet. Most people hold the hook and yarn as they would a pencil or a knife, but you should experiment to find the most comfortable way for you.

Mastering the slipknot

Making a slipknot is the first step in any project. Master the slipknot technique, and you are on your way to super crochet!

Make a loop in the yarn. With your hook, catch the ball end of the yarn and draw it through the loop. Pull firmly on the yarn and hook to tighten the knot and create your first loop.

Making a chain

1. Before making a chain, you need to place the slipknot on a hook. To make a chain, hold the tail end of the yarn with the left hand and bring the yarn over the hook by passing the hook in front of the yarn, under, and around it.

2. Keeping the tension in the yarn taut, draw the hook and yarn through the loop.

3. Pull the yarn, hook it through the hole, and begin again, ensuring that the stitches are fairly loose. Repeat to make the number of chains required. As the chain lengthens, keep hold of the bottom edge to maintain the tension.

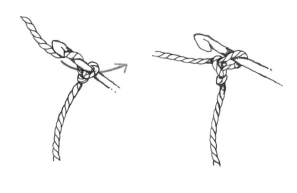

How to count a chain

To count the stitches, use the right side of the chain, or the side that has more visible and less twisted "V" shapes, as shown. Do not count the original slip stitch, but count each "V" as one chain.

Making a slip stitch (sl st)

A slip stitch is used to join one stitch to another or a stitch to another point, as in joining a circle, and is usually made by picking up two strands of a stitch. However, where it is worked into the starting chain, only pick up the back loop.

1. Insert the hook into the back loop of the next stitch and pass yarn over hook (yo), as in the chain stitch.

2. Draw yarn through both loops of stitch.

The magic ring: working in the round

There are two ways to start circular crochet. One is with a chain and another is with a loop. A loop, or magic ring, is the more usual way to make amigurumi. This way of working in the round ensures that there is no hole in the middle of the work, as there is with a chain ring, because the central hole is adjustable and can be pulled tightly closed.

Let's make a magic ring

This will be the first round of your amigurumi, so you need to master it!

1. Make a loop by wrapping the yarn twice onto your forefinger, with the tail end of the yarn on the right, the ball end on the left.

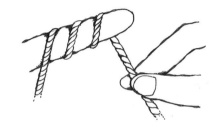

2. Pull the ball end through the loop (steady your work with your hand).

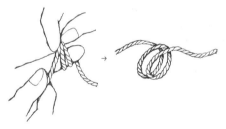

3. Make one chain (ch) through the loop on the hook you have drawn through to secure the round.

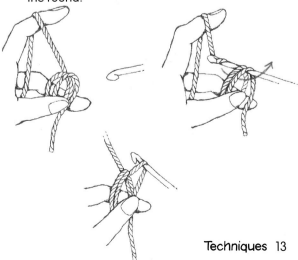

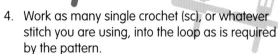

4. Work as many single crochet (sc), or whatever stitch you are using, into the loop as is required by the pattern.

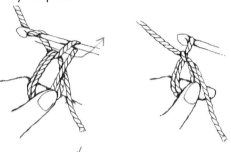

5. Pull the last stitch out long enough so that it won't come undone. Find out which loop will be tightened first by pulling one of the loops.

6. Pull this loop as tight as you can.

7. Pull the tail end of the yarn to tighten up the whole loop. Now you have no hole in the middle of the first round.

 →

Completing the magic ring: first round

Insert the hook into the first stitch of a magic ring and pull the yarn through all the way.

This is called "slip stitch" (sl st).

Start the second round

To crochet a flat circle, you need to keep working in the round with increasing stitches.

1. Make one chain (ch). Insert the hook into the first stitch of a circle, and put the yarn over the hook (yo) and then draw the yarn through the loop. This is called single crochet (sc). In amigurumi, this is the technique you will use the most.

2. Add one more sc into the same stitch. This is called increasing (inc).

Repeat 1 and 2 into every stitch and you will finish the second round with twice the number of stitches.

On the second round, increase in alternate stitches.

Third round: 1 sc into each of the next 2 stitches, 2 sc into the next one. Repeat.

Fourth round: 1 sc into each of the next 3 stitches, 2 sc into the next one. Repeat.

The more rounds you go, the more stitches you need to make between increases.

Unless otherwise stated, close each round with a slip stitch. Make 1 chain to lift your hook to the height of the next round. (This chain does not count as a stitch).

Making a chain ring

1. Work a chain as long as required by the pattern.

2. Join the last chain to the first with a slip stitch (sl st). Begin the first round by working into each chain stitch.

Variety of stitches

Single crochet (sc): the main stitch used for amigurumi

1. Insert the hook, front to back, into the next stitch. Yo.

2. Draw through one loop to front; there should be two loops on the hook. Yo.

3. Draw through both loops to complete single crochet.

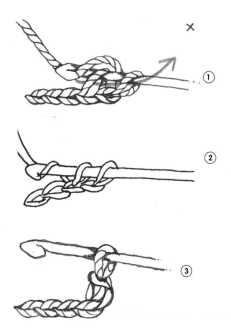

Double crochet (dc)

This makes a more open fabric as the stitches are taller.

1. Wrap the yarn over the hook (yo) from back to front. Insert the hook into the next stitch, from front to back. Yo again and draw through the stitch.

2. There should be three loops on the hook. Yo and pull through two loops. Yo and draw through first two.

3. There should be two loops on the hook. Yo. Pull through the remaining two loops. Yo and draw through last two to complete.

Half-double crochet (hdc)

The half-double is simply that: half of a double crochet. Therefore, the stitch is slightly shorter than double crochet. In step 2 of double crochet, pull through all the remaining loops in one movement.

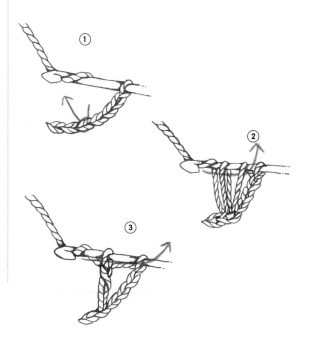

Fastening Off

When you've finished crocheting your tasty treats, fastening off is the next most important step. After that, all you need to do is fill it with stuffing and stitch the parts together.

Here are some useful things to remember:

When you fasten off the end of a part that is going to be stitched to another part, leave a long tail for sewing the two together. Do not weave this end in.

Connect two pieces by taking stitches alternately from each piece and fastening them securely.

Fastening off

1. After working the last stitch, snip off the yarn from the ball, leaving a length of a few centimeters to weave in.

2. Draw through the last loop, pulling tightly to fasten.

Weaving in ends

1. Use the hook to draw the yarn through at least five stitches, weaving the yarn over and under as you go to secure the yarn and ensure it does not work free.

2. Snip off the excess yarn.

When fastening off, leave openings for stuffing where appropriate. Stuff firmly, sew up gaps, and embroider details as shown in the illustrations.

Creating Tasty Cute Treats

There aren't really any hard-and-fast rules when it comes to designing amigurumi. Once you've mastered the basic stitches and practiced the technique of working in the round, you're bound to be inspired to start inventing your own crocheted creations. In this book you will find 25 patterns for all sorts of different foods — from sushi to salads, from cookies to candies, and from fruit to fries. But there are so many more tasty treats out there to inspire you — so get out the crochet hook and start cooking!

Developing a design

I love cooking and I love crochet, so when I was asked to do this book I was so happy!

I'd already created a complete Christmas dinner — with all the trimmings — and a beautiful wedding cake for a special friend, but I jumped at the chance to make even more foody amigurumi.

So when I knew I was going to start creating new designs I went to the best place possible for ideas: cook books!

In cook books you can find lots of lovely pictures of yummy food without having to buy or make the dishes! You can also look on the Internet for inspiring pictures — search recipe websites or browse the online food shops.

Don't be put off by complicated dishes — remember, you can make things in several parts and then stitch them all together later. Lots of food is round and so amigurumi techniques are perfect. But don't be afraid to try making other shapes too.

Sketching

When I have an idea, I start by making a sketch. It might be just a pencil drawing or something more complicated, with colors added. You don't have to be good at drawing to do this; sometimes just a brief drawing of a shape and a little scribble of some details is enough to help you envisage the finished shape of your amigurumi, and to help you get started with the stitching.

Choosing materials

There are lots of lovely brightly colored foods
and dishes so there is plenty of opportunity to
get out some colorful yarns. Bright greens, rosy
reds, and sunshine yellows can all appear in our
favorite foods.

The choice of materials is endless. By playing with
a variety of materials, you'll discover interesting
differences in your finished result. Experiment with
fancy yarns — yarns with touches of glitter and fluff
— to create interesting, tasty textures.

Making shapes

This section will show you how to create some of the basic shapes for your projects. A lot of these shapes can be twisted and folded, or stitched to other shapes to create new ones.

Once you've mastered these, you can change the shapes to create all kinds of different foods!

Teardrop shapes

This type of shape is really simple. Just make a disc in the size you want, then continue with sc until the section is the length you require.

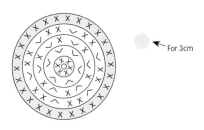

← For 3cm

Disc shapes

These are very simple to make. Start with the magic circle and then keep increasing stitches until the disc is the size you want. To make circular treats, make two discs, stitch together and stuff. To make semicircular items, fold a disc in half before stitching and stuffing.

Ball shapes

Start with a disc shape, and then keep increasing stitches until the disc is the size of sphere you want to make. Continue for a couple of rounds without shaping, and then start decreasing.

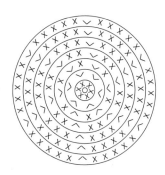

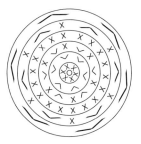

Rectangles and squares

These are probably the easiest shapes to make. Start with a basic chain and then work crochet stitches along it. Turn the work at the end of the row and then work back along it. Keep going until you've got a piece the size you want. Squares and rectangles can be folded, bent, or rolled into different shapes.

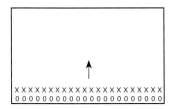

Rectangles with curved corners

To make this type of shape, start with a chain and work one row of stitches, just as for an ordinary square or rectangle. Then instead of turning the work and crocheting in rows, you work into the first chain, making stitches in the underside of the chain. To make sure the shape lies flat, you need to make at least three stitches in the first and last chains of the foundation chain.

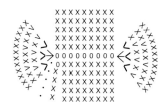

Rhomboid shapes

This four-sided shape looks like a sloping rectangle. It's useful for making twisted shapes. Start with a foundation chain as you would for a square or rectangle and then decrease by two stitches (sc2tog) at the beginning of the first row, and increase (2sc into same st) at the end of the row. On the next row, increase at the beginning and decrease at the end. Continue working, increasing and decreasing in the same way until the shape is as big as you need.

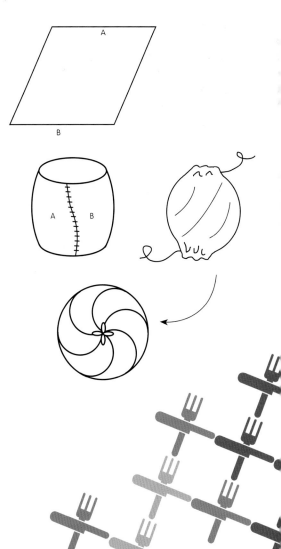

Chapter 1

Fast
Food
Favorites

Wow, Wow, Sushi!

From the home of amigurumi comes sushi, probably the prettiest fast food around. These Japanese snack-sized morsels are the smart choice when it comes to lunch on the run. This sushi looks – literally – too good to eat!

Materials

HOOK SIZE: C

YARN: various different colors, depending on which sushi you would like to make.

Here I've used: white, red, yellow, black, pink, light green, dark green, purple.

Rice

← for 5cm

Use white yarn.

Make a loop with the tail end of the yarn on the right, keeping the ball end on the left.

Pull the ball end through the loop.

Make one ch through the loop on the hook you have drawn through to secure the circle.

Work 6sc into the circle and complete the circle with sl st into the first sc.

1st round: 2sc into each sc.

2nd round: *1sc, 2sc into next sc. *6 times.

Work 1sc in each st until piece is 2in long.

Next round: *1sc in next st, sc2tog in next st. Repeat from * to end.

Next round: sc2tog to end.

Stuff it to make your sushi base. Fasten off. You will later sew the tuna, egg or shrimp sushi on top.

Now you can start to order your sushi!

Clockwise from top left to right: Ikura and cucumber, rolled sushi, tuna, egg, shrimp, and octopus!

Tuna

Use red yarn.

Ch14; turn.

1st row: ch1; 1sc in all sts to end.

Repeat for 18 rows. Fasten off.

Fold it in half and stitch both ends together.

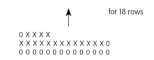

for 18 rows

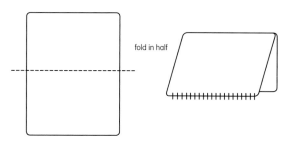

fold in half

Egg

Use yellow yarn.

Follow the same pattern as for the tuna, above.

To make seaweed (nori) band around the sushi, with black yarn, ch4; turn.

1st row: ch1; 1sc in all sts to end.

Repeat 1st row until the work is enough long to wrap around the egg and rice. Fasten off.

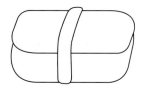

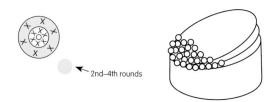

2nd–4th rounds

Ikura and cucumber

For the ikura (salmon roe), use pink yarn.

Make a loop with the tail end of the yarn on the right, keeping the ball end on the left.

Pull the ball end through the loop.

Make one ch through the loop on the hook you have drawn through to secure the circle.

Work 6sc into the circle and complete the circle with sl st into the first sc.

1st round: 2sc into each of the 6sc.

1sc into all sts for 3 rounds.

Fasten off and gather it up.

You need to make at least 5 of them!

To make the cucumber, use a light and a dark green yarn. Start with the light green.

Make a circle as for Ikura; 6sc into the circle to start.

1st round: 2sc into each of the 6sc.

2nd round: 3sc into each of the first 2sc, 4sc, 3sc into each of the next 2sc, 4sc.

Change yarn color to darker green for the cucumber skin.

3rd round: 1sc in all sts.

Fasten off.

To make the seaweed to wrap around sushi, use black yarn, make ch22; turn.

1st row: ch1; 1sc in all sts to end.

Repeat until work measures 1½in.

Fasten off.

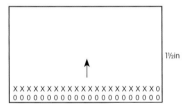

Sew the top and bottom of the strip together and then join along one long edge. Insert a little stuffing and attach the cucumber to one end of the seaweed wrap. Sew the ikura onto the cucumber, toward the other end of the seaweed wrap.

Shrimp

With white yarn, ch9; turn.

1st row: ch1; 1sc in all sts to end.

Repeat for 10 more rows, changing yarn color from red to white for every two rows.

12th row: sc2tog, 1sc to last 2sc, sc2tog.

13th & 14th rows: As row 12.

15th row: 3dc into the first sc, 2dc in next sc, 3dc into the last sc.

Fasten off.

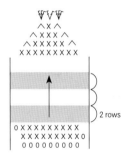

Rolled sushi

← 4th–8th rounds

Use dark and light green, yellow, white, pink and black yarn.

Using dark green yarn, make a loop with the tail end of the yarn on the right, keeping the ball end on the left.

Pull the ball end through the loop.

Make one ch through the loop on the hook you have drawn through to secure the circle.

Work 6sc into the circle and complete the circle with sl st into the first sc.

After the first 3sc in dark green, switch to a light green for last 3sc.

1st round: Change to yellow; 2sc into each of the first 3sc; change to white; 2sc into the next sc; change to pink; 2sc into each of the next 2sc.)

2nd round: Change to white; *1sc, 2sc into next sc. *6 times.

3rd round: *1sc into each of two sc, 2sc into next sc. *6 times.

4th round: Change to black (for the seaweed), 1sc in each st.

5th–8th rounds: as 4th round.

Fasten off.

Make another piece like this for bottom, but working only rounds 1 to 4. Fasten off.

Stuff it to make a sushi base.

Sew the first disc to the bottom to complete.

Octopus

With white yarn, ch9; turn.

1st row: 1sc into the second sc, 1sc in all sts to end; turn.

2nd row: ch1, 2sc in all sts to end; turn.

3rd row: Change to purple yarn. ch1, 4dc into every sc to end.

Fasten off.

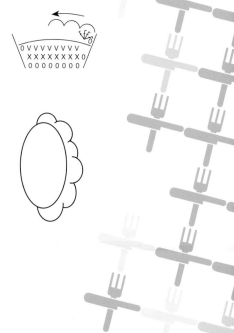

Pickled ginger

With pink yarn, ch15; turn.

1st row: ch1, 1sc in all sts to end; turn.

2nd–4th rows: as 1st row.

5th row: 5dc into every sc, then fasten off.

Roll it and place it with your sushi delight set!

Don't forget, you'll need chopsticks and some soy sauce to complete your tasty meal.

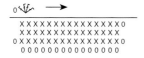

15sts

Green zigzag decoration

With dark green yarn, ch18; turn.

1st row: ch1, 1sc in all stitches to end; turn.

2nd–6th rows: as 1st row.

7th row: ch1, 1sc into each of next 4sc, sc2tog, turn.

8th row: ch1, skip 2sc, 1sc into each of next 3sc, turn.

9th row: ch1, sc2tog, fasten off. Rejoin yarn to the left of the last stitch worked on the 7th row.

Repeat 7th to 9th rows. Rejoin yarn to the left of the last stitch worked on the 7th row.

Work the 7th row. Work one row of sc before working the 8th row.

Work one row of sc before working the 9th row. Fasten off.

Pizza to Go

For dinner with a difference, grab a slice of this Italian speciality. With a traditional, tricolor-style topping of soft mozzarella, big beefy tomatoes, and sprigs of basil – not forgetting the black olives – this perfect pizza is the best of bella Italia.

Materials

HOOK SIZE: C

YARN: Light brown yarn for pizza base

Mix dark brown yarn for pizza crust

Dark red yarn for pizza sauce

Bright red yarn for tomato slices

White yarn for melted cheese

Green yarn for basil leaves

Black yarn for olive slices

Structure

This yummy, bite-sized pizza is basically made up of two parts.

Part A is the pizza base, and part B is the same sort of shape, for the tomato sauce.

You need to make 8 of each slice to complete the whole pizza.

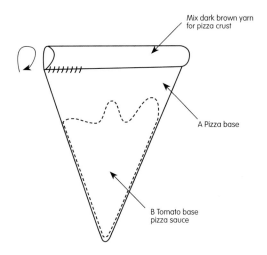

Mix dark brown yarn for pizza crust

A Pizza base

B Tomato base pizza sauce

Pizza base (part A)

```
X X X X X X X X X X X X X X 0
0 X X X X X X X X X X X X X      ⎞
X X X X X X X X X X X X X 0      ⎟  Brown for crust
0 X X X X X X X X X X X X        ⎠
V X X X X X X X X X X V 0
0 X X X X X X X X X X X
  V X X X X X X X X V 0
  0 X X X X X X X X X
  V X X X X X X X V 0
    0 X X X X X X X
    X X X X X X X 0
    0 X X X X X X X
      V X X X X V 0
      0 V X V
        V 0
        0
```

With light brown yarn, ch2; turn.

1st row: 2sc in the second chain from hook; turn. (3sts)

2nd row: ch1, 2sc in the first sc, 1sc, 2sc in next sc, turn.

3rd row: ch1, 2sc in first sc, 1sc in next three sc, 2sc in next sc, turn.

4th–6th row: ch1, 1sc in all, turn.

7th row: ch1, 2sc in next st, 1sc in each st to last sc, 2sc in last st, turn.

8th row: ch1, 1sc in all, turn.

9th row: ch1, 2sc in next sc, 1sc until last sc, 2sc in next sc, turn.

10th row: ch1, 1sc in all, turn.

11th row: ch1, 2sc in next sc, 1sc until last sc, 2sc in next sc, turn.

12th row: Starting using a dark brown yarn and, working with both yarns at once, ch1, 1sc in all, turn.

13th–16th row: as for row 12, turn.

Fasten off. Roll 3 rows inwards to make an edge for the pizza and stitch down on to the base

Tomato sauce (part B)

With the red yarn, follow the same pattern as for the pizza base but when you reach the 6th row, make a few random sc, dc, or hdc along the row to give it a wiggly edge. This will make it look like the tomato sauce has been artfully spread.

Stitch the tomato sauce on to the pizza base.

Tomato slice

Using bright red yarn, ch6. Join with sl st to first ch to make a circle.

1st round: 1sc in each ch (6sts).

2nd round: ch9, skip 1sc, 1dc into next sc, ch6, skip 1sc, 1dc to next sc, ch5, sl st into the 4th chain from beginning, to complete the circle.

3rd round: 1sc in each ch.

Fasten off.

Olive slice

Using black yarn, ch6. Join with sl st to first ch to make a circle.

1st round: 1sc in each ch (6sts).

Fasten off.

Basil

Using green yarn, make ch6; turn.

1st row: 1sc into the second ch, 1hdc, 1dc, 1hdc, 1sc.

Fasten off.

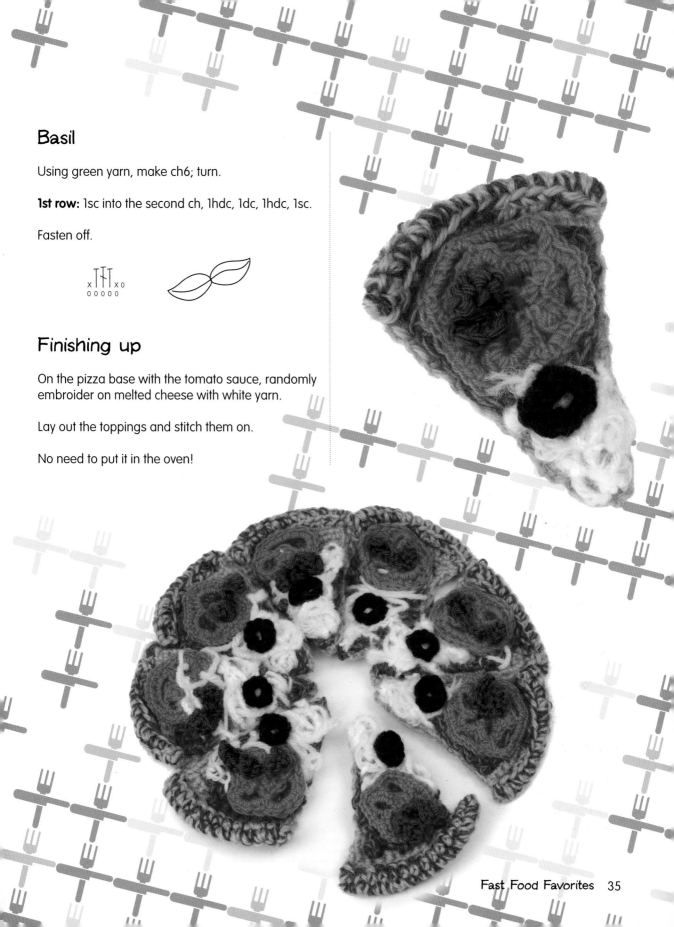

Finishing up

On the pizza base with the tomato sauce, randomly embroider on melted cheese with white yarn.

Lay out the toppings and stitch them on.

No need to put it in the oven!

Yum-yum Burger

You've got to pile up the toppings if you want to make the best burger in town, so sandwich a big juicy burger between two buns with lots of lettuce and a slice of tomato. Add a few more layers to make a real super-size meal.

Materials

HOOK SIZE: C

YARN: Light brown yarn and white yarn for burger buns

Red yarn for tomato

Light and dark green yarn for fresh lettuce

Dark brown yarn for burger

Structure

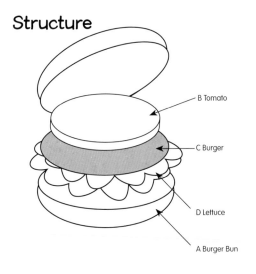

- B Tomato
- C Burger
- D Lettuce
- A Burger Bun

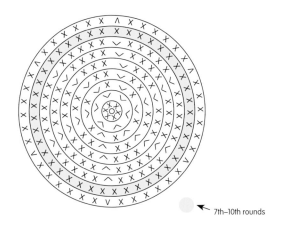

← 7th–10th rounds

Burger buns (part A)

Use light brown yarn.

Make a loop with the tail end of the yarn on the right, keeping the ball end on the left.

Pull the ball end through the loop.

Make one ch through the loop on the hook you have drawn through to secure the circle.

Work 6sc into the circle and complete the circle with sl st into the first sc.

1st round: 2sc into each sc.

2nd round: *1sc, 2sc into next sc. *6 times.

3rd round: *2sc, 2sc into next sc. *6 times.

4th round: *3sc, 2sc to next sc. *6 times.

5th round: *4sc, 2sc to next sc. *6 times.

6th round: *5sc, 2sc to next sc. *6 times.

7th–10th round: 1sc in all.

11th round: *5sc, 2sc together. *6 times.

Fasten off.

Make two.

Using white yarn, follow the same pattern above but without the last 5 rounds. Make two for the underside of the buns.

Sew a white part to a brown part for both the top and the bottom of the bun, remembering to insert stuffing before finishing the seam.

You can embroider some sesame seeds on the top half of the bun.

Tomato (part B)

Use red yarn.

Make a loop with the tail end of the yarn on the right, keeping the ball end on the left.

Pull the ball end through the loop.

Make one ch through the loop on the hook you have drawn through to secure the circle.

Work 6sc into the circle and complete the circle with sl st into the first sc.

1st round: 2sc into each sc.

2nd round: *1sc, 2sc into next sc. *6 times.

3rd round: *2sc, 2sc into next sc. *6 times.

4th round: *3sc, 2sc into next sc. *6 times.

5th round: *4sc, 2sc into next sc. * 6 times.

6th–7th round: *1sc in all.

Fasten off.

Make two, stuff them, and stitch together.

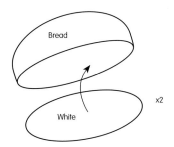

6th–7th rounds

Burger (part C)

Use dark brown yarn.

Make a loop with the tail end of the yarn on the right, keeping the ball end on the left.

Pull the ball end through the loop.

Make one ch through the loop on the hook you have drawn through to secure the circle.

Work 6sc into the circle and complete the circle with sl st into the first sc.

1st round: 2sc into each sc.

2nd round: *1sc, 2sc into next sc. *6 times.

3rd round: *2sc, 2sc into next sc. *6 times.

4th round: *3sc, 2sc into next sc. *6 times.

5th round: *4sc, 2sc into next sc. *6 times.

6th round: *5sc, 2sc into next sc. *6 times.

7th–9th round: 1sc in all.

Fasten off.

Make two, stuff them, and stitch together.

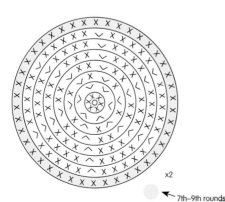

x2

7th–9th rounds

Lettuce (part D)

With green yarn, make ch12.

1st round: ch1, 1sc into each st along both sides of the chain, join with a sl st.

2nd round: ch2, 3hdc in each st around, join with a sl st in first hdc.

3rd round: ch3, 4dc into all stitches around, join with a sl st in first dc.

Fasten off.

Make at least 3, and vary the color of the green yarn for different types of lettuce.

Tasty Hot Dog

If you want fast food, then a tasty hot dog is just for you. Why not whip up a wiener just like this one and then grab a bun to go – make sure you don't forget the mustard and ketchup!

Materials

HOOK SIZE: C

YARN: White yarn and light brown yarn for bun

Dark brown yarn for hot dog

Red yarn and yellow yarn for ketchup and mustard

Bun

Using light brown yarn, ch18; 1sc into the second ch from hook, 1sc in each of next 15sts, 2sc in last st, continue working 1sc in all sts along unused side of foundation chain to last st, 2sc in last st. Start working in the round.

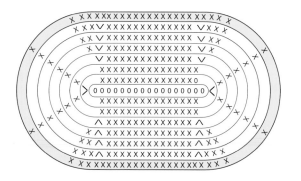

1st round: *1sc into each of next 17sc, 2sc in next sc. Repeat from *.

2nd round: 2sc into next sc, 1sc into each of next 15sc, 2sc into next sc, 1sc into each of next 2sc, 2sc into next sc, 1sc into each of next 15sc, 2sc into next sc, 1sc into each of next 2sc.

3rd round: 1sc, 2sc into next st, 1sc into each of next 15sc, 2sc into next sc, 1sc into each of next 4sc, 2sc into next sc, 1sc into each of next 15sc, 2sc into next sc, 1sc into each of 3sc.

4th round: 1sc in each of next 2sc, 2sc into next sc, 1sc into each of next 15sc, 2sc into next sc, 1sc to each of next 6sc, 2sc into next sc, 1sc into each of next 16sc, 2sc into next sc, 1sc to each of next 4sc.

5th round: 1sc in each of next 3sc, 2sc into next sc, 1sc into each of next 15sc, 2sc into next sc, 1sc to each of next 8sc, 2sc into next sc, 1sc into each of next 16sc, 2sc into next sc, 1sc to each of next 5sc.

Next round: 1sc into all sc for 1¼in.

Fasten off.

Make two of these using the light brown yarn.

With the white yarn, make another two as above, but without the last 1¼in of sc (so you just have flat ovals).

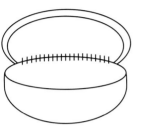
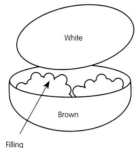

White

Brown

Filling

Hot Dog

Use the dark brown yarn.

Make a loop with the tail end of the yarn on the right, keeping the ball end on the left.

Pull the ball end through the loop.

Make one ch through the loop on the hook you have drawn through to secure the circle.

Work 6sc into the circle and complete the circle with sl st into the first sc.

1st round: *1sc, 2sc into next sc. *6 times.

2nd round: 1sc in all.

Repeat round 2 until the work is long enough to make a hot dog to fit the roll.

Last round: *1sc, sc2tog together. *3 times.

Fasten off.

If you like tasty condiments on your hot dog, chain stitch the ketchup and mustard using the red and yellow yarn over the top of the hot dog.

No-fat Fries

"Do you want fries with that?" If you do, then try this take out with a twist – totally fat-free fries. You can make as many as you like and you won't have to worry about weight gain!

Materials

HOOK SIZE: C

YARN: Red yarn for the bag

Yellow yarn for embroidering letter

Cream yarn for the fries

Bag

Using red yarn, make ch16; turn.

1st row: 1sc in second ch from hook, 1sc in each ch to end; turn.

Work 4–6in in rows of sc.

(You can make the piece longer, and wider.)

Fasten off.

Using the yellow yarn and chain stitch, embroider an initial on to the top half of the finished piece.

Fold it in half and stitch along both sides to make small bag. Leave a small section at the top unstitched so you can turn over the edge.

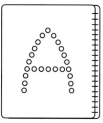

Fries

Using cream yarn, ch30 and work as for 1st row of bag.

Fasten off

Make as many fries as you like so they fit into the bag. You can make some longer, and some shorter – just like real fries!

Chapter 2

Scrumptious Cakes and Desserts

Best-ever Cherry Pie

When you want a break, why not take time out for a cup of tea and a nice slice of pie? So put the kettle on, get out your best china, and try this fruity delight. It's as easy as pie!

Materials

HOOK SIZE: C

YARN: Light brown for crust

Brown yarn for lattice

Dark red for cherry filling

Cream for whipped cream topping

```
x Ψ x Ψ x Ψ x Ψ x Ψ x Ψ x Ψ 0
0 X X X X X X X X X X X X
X X X X X X X X X X X X 0
0 X X X X X X X X X X X X
X X X X X X X X X X X X 0
0 X X X X X X X X X X X X
V X X X X X X X X X X X 0
0 X X X X X X X X X X
X X X X X X X X X X 0
0 X X X X X X X X V
X X X X X X X X 0
0 X X X X X X X V
X X X X X X X 0
0 X X X X X V
X X X X X 0
0 X X X V
X X X 0
0 X V
V 0
0
```

Base Crust

With light brown yarn, make ch1; turn.

1st row: 2sc into the ch1, turn.

2nd row: ch1, 1sc, 2sc into next st, turn.

3rd row: ch1, 1sc in all sts, turn. (4sts)

4th row: ch1, 3sc, 2sc into last st, turn.

5th row: ch1, 1sc in all sts, turn. (6sts)

6th row: ch1, 5sc, 2sc into last st, turn.

7th row: ch1, 1sc in all sts, turn. (8sts)

8th row: ch1, 7sc, 2sc into last st, turn.

9th row: ch1, 1sc in all sts, turn. (10sts)

10th row: ch1, 9sc, 2sc into last st, turn.

11th row: ch1, 1sc in all sts, turn. (12sts)

12th row: As row 11.

13th row: ch1, 11sc, 2sc into last st, turn.

14th row: ch1, 1sc in all sts, turn. (14sts)

15th–18th row: As row 14.

19th row: ch1, *3dc into first st, 1sc in next st. Repeat from * to end.

Fasten off.

For the top crust, make another piece but without the last 4 rows.

Cherry filling

The cherry filling is made in two parts, to form the sides of the pie.

With dark red yarn, make a ch as long as one side of the top crust.

1st row: 1sc in 2nd ch from hook, 1sc in all sts to end, turn.

2nd row: ch3, *1dc into back loop of next st, dc5tog into back loop of next st (makes 1 bobble). Repeat from * to end.

Fasten off.

Make another one for the other side.

Lattice

With dark brown yarn, make a ch long enough to go diagonally across the top of the pie.

1st row: 1sc in 2nd ch from hook, 1sc in all sts to end.

Fasten off.

Make more, in different lengths, to create the lattice pattern across the top.

Whipped cream

With creamy colored yarn, ch15; turn.

1st row: 1hdc into back loop of second chain from the hook, *1sc into back loop of next ch. Repeat from * to end. Turn.

2nd row: ch3, *1sc in the back loop only of each st along row.

Repeat 2nd row twice, fasten off.

Roll it into a shape that looks like whipped cream and stitch in place.

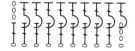

Finishing up

Fold up the edge of the pie base to form the crust, sew a length of pie filling to the base and crust, forming one side. Repeat with the other piece of pie filling.

Sew the lattice pieces to the pie top. Sew on the whipped cream. Sew the pie top to the cherry-filling sides, leaving a gap for the stuffing. Stuff and then sew up the gap.

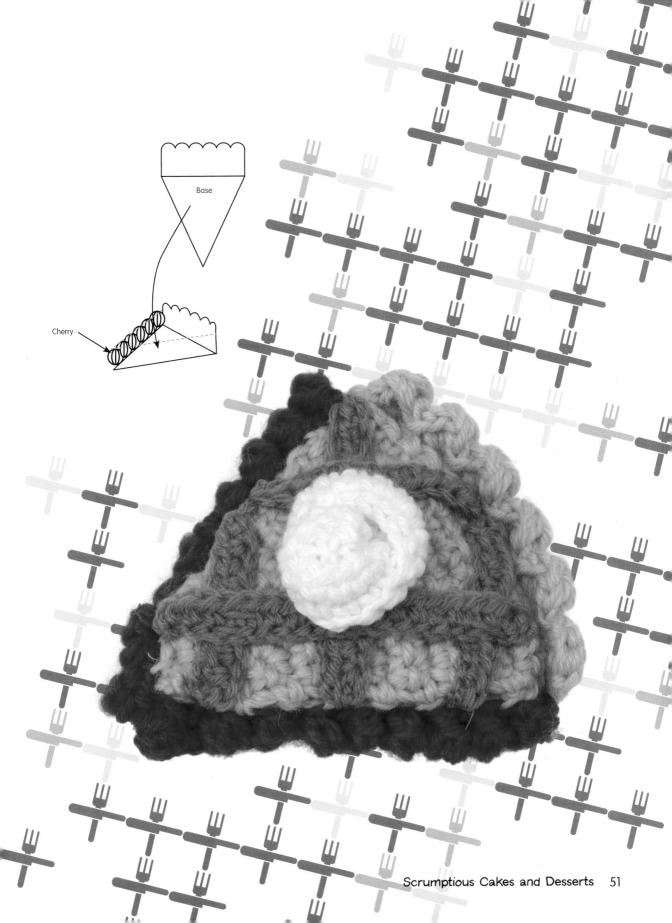

Base

Cherry

Cute Cupcakes

When it's your birthday what could be better than a cake with candles? Well, lots of cakes with candles, of course! So if you're having a party, make a cute cupcake for each guest and everyone has a happy keepsake to take home.

Materials

HOOK SIZE: C

YARN: White yarn for cupcake cases

Blue yarn and bright orange yarn for edge of cases

Brown tweed-effect or bouclé yarn for cakes

Small amounts of brightly colored yarns for decoration

Red mohair yarn for candle flame

White yarn, pink yarn and bright blue yarn for candles

Structure

The cute cupcake is made up from two parts – the top of the cake and the cupcake case.

Getting the balance between the cake size and the case size is the key to making your cupcake look truly perfect!

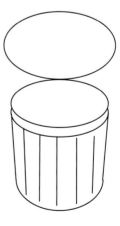

Cupcake case

As you can see, the case has a ribbed texture.

Using white yarn, ch12; turn.

1st row: 1hdc into fourth ch from hook, *1hdc into next st. Repeat from * to end, turn.

2nd row: ch2, *1hdc around the stem of next st on the row below, from the front of the work. Repeat * to end, turn.

3rd row: ch2, *1hdc around the stem of next st on the row below, from the back of the work. Repeat from * to end, turn.

Repeat rows 2 and 3 until the work measures 9in.

Fasten off.

Stitch the beginning and end edges together to create a cylinder.

This is the outside of the case. You will also need to make a base.

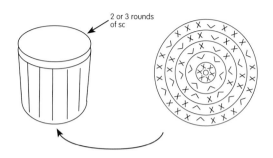

2 or 3 rounds of sc

Base

Using white yarn, make a loop with the tail end of the yarn on the right, keeping the ball end on the left.

Pull the ball end through the loop.

Make one chain through loop on hook you have drawn through to secure the circle.

Work 6sc into the circle and complete the circle with sl st into the first sc.

1st round: 2sc into each st.

2nd round: *1sc, 2sc into next st. *6 times.

3rd round: *2sc, 2sc into next st. *6 times.

4th round: *3sc, 2sc into next st. *6 times.

Fasten off.

Stitch this base to the bottom of the cupcake case.

Join a different colored yarn to the top edge of the case and work in sc all around; join with a sl st to first sc. Work another 1 or 2 rounds of sc as desired to give the case a decorative edge.

Cake

Using brown tweed-effect or bouclé yarn, make a loop with the tail end of the yarn on the right, keeping the ball end on the left.

Pull the ball end through the loop.

Make one ch through the loop on the hook you have drawn through to secure the circle.

Work 6sc into the circle and complete the circle with sl st into the first sc.

1st round: 2sc into each st.

2nd round: *1sc, 2sc into next st. *6 times.

3rd round: *2sc, 2sc into next st. *6 times.

4th round: *3sc, 2sc into next st. *6 times.

5th round: *4sc, 2sc into next st. *6 times.

6th–9th rounds: 1sc in all.

Fasten off.

Candle

Starting with white yarn, ch10; turn.

1st row: 2sc into the first st, 7sc, sc2tog, turn.

2nd row: ch1, sc2tog, 6sc, 2sc into last st, turn.

3rd row: Change to pink yarn; ch1, 2sc into the first st, 6sc, sc2tog, turn.

Repeat rows 2 and 3 until work measures 1¾in, changing color on the odd-numbered rows.

Fasten off.

Stitch both top and bottom ends together and you will see diagonal stripes running around the candle body. Make another candle with blue stripes.

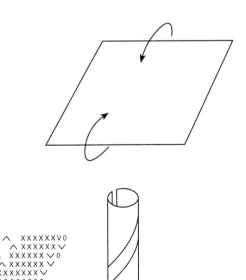

6th–9th rounds

Flame

Use red mohair.

Make a loop with the tail end of the yarn on the right, keeping the ball end on the left.

Pull the ball end through the loop.

Make one ch through the loop on the hook you have drawn through to secure the circle.

Work 6sc into the circle and complete the circle with sl st into the first sc.

1st round: 2sc into each 6sc.

2nd round: 1sc in all sts.

3rd & 4th rounds: As round 2.

5th round: *1sc, sc2tog. *6 times.

6th round: 1sc in all sts.

7th round: *sc2tog in all sts.

Fasten off.

Stuff the candle body and flame, then stitch the flame onto the body.

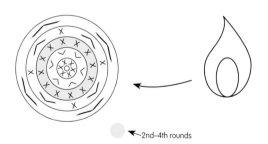

←—2nd–4th rounds

Finishing up

Sew the case and the cake top together, leaving a gap for stuffing. Stuff and then sew up the gap.

Using lengths of brightly colored yarn, decorate the cake with pretty toppings made by chain-stitching small dots and circles.

Dinky Doughnuts

These dinky doughnuts are sure to please when it comes to a take-away treat. Covered in sugary frosting, they're everyone's favorite treat. But when you pick up coffee and a cake to go, just remember not to dunk these crocheted creations!

Materials

HOOK SIZE: C

YARN: Brown yarn for doughnuts

Colorful yarns for decoration and icing.

Structure

The simple doughnut is made from a jellyfish-type shape, sewn inside out (if you can picture this!)

Make part A first. This is made by starting at the inner edge of the shape and working outward.

Part A will be the base for the doughnut and is made in brown yarn, so part B can be crocheted in any color you like for the icing.

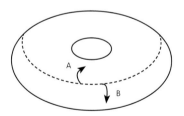

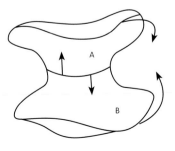

Part A

Using brown yarn, make ch18. Join with a sl st to first ch to make a circle.

1st round: 1sc in all sts, finishing with sl st to first st.

2nd–4th rounds: As round 1.

5th round: *1sc, 2sc into the next st. *9 times.

6th round: *2sc, 2sc into the next st. *9 times.

7th round: *3sc, 2sc into the next st. *9 times.

8th–11th rounds: As round 1.

Fasten off.

Part B

Using your chosen color for icing, join the yarn to the starting point of part A.

1st round: *1sc, 2sc into next st. *9 times.

2nd–6th rounds: Repeat rounds 5–9 of part A.

Fasten off.

Finishing up

Sew the outer edges of the parts A and B together, leaving a gap for stuffing. Stuff and then sew up the gap.

Rejoin the icing-color yarn at the seam and work a round of random sc, hdc, dc, hdc, and sc. This will give the icing a scalloped edge and look as if it is dripping down the doughnut!

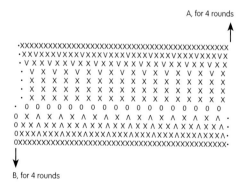

A, for 4 rounds

B, for 4 rounds

Swirly Cream Roll

Get really creative and make this creamy cake. Packed full of swirly sweetness, and topped with fondant and cream, it's a sure winner at the dessert table. And don't forget a cherry on the top for that perfect finishing flourish.

Materials

HOOK SIZE: C

YARN: Light brown yarn for cake

Brown yarn for chocolate

White yarn for cream

Red yarn for cherry

Structure

To make the tasty rolled cake, you will need 4 parts.

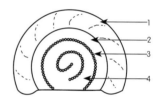

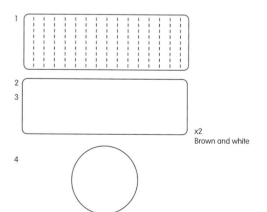

x2
Brown and white

Part 1

Using light brown yarn, ch14; turn.

1st row: 1hdc in 4th ch from hook, 1hdc in all sts to end, turn.

2nd row: ch2, *1hdc around the stem of next st on the row below, from the front of the work. Repeat * to end, turn.

3rd row: ch2, *1hdc around the stem of next st on the row below, from the back of the work. Repeat from * to end, turn.

Repeat rows 2 and 3 until work measures 8in.

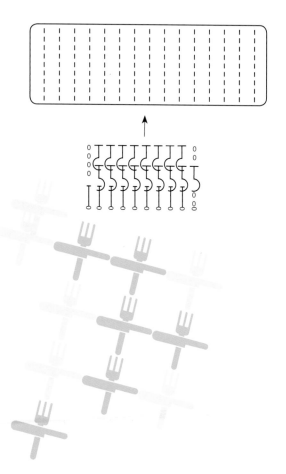

Parts 2 and 3

These parts make the cream inside. Using white yarn, ch16; turn.

1st row: 1hdc in 3rd ch from hook, 1hdc in all sts to end, turn.

Repeat row 1 until the work is as long as part 1.

Make another identical piece in brown.

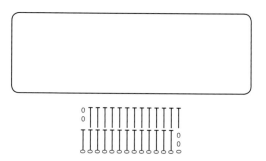

Part 4

This will be the center of the cake. Put parts 2 and 3 together and roll into a cylinder. Wrap part 1 around the outside; sew in place. Part 4 needs to be big enough to fit into your roll.

Using white yarn, make a loop with the tail end of the yarn on the right, keeping the ball end on the left.

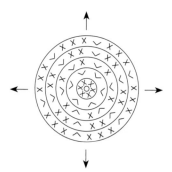

Pull the ball end through the loop.

Make one ch through the loop on the hook you have drawn through to secure the circle.

Work 6sc into the circle and complete the circle with sl st into the first sc.

1st round: 2sc into each 6sc.

2nd round: *1sc, 2sc into next st. *6 times.

3rd round: *2sc, 2sc into next st. *6 times.

4th round: *3sc, 2sc into next st. *6 times.

Continue working rounds, increasing in the same way, until part 4 is big enough to fit the side of the cylinder. Fasten off.

Chain stitch a swirly line of chocolate on to part 4. Repeat to make another piece, making sure to match the way the chocolate chain curls.

Whipped cream

Work as for the whipped cream for the cherry pie - see page 50.

Chocolate sauce

Using brown yarn, work as for the whipped cream.

Cherry

Using red yarn, work as for the pea - see page 126.

Finishing up

Sew the chocolate sauce and whipped cream in place on top of the cylinder made from parts 1, 2, and 3.

Sew the cherry on top.

Sew one part 4 on one end of the cylinder. Add stuffing, then sew the other part 4 on the other side of the cylinder.

So-good Sundae

Pull out all the stops with this sweet treat. Pile up the ice cream, the chocolate sauce, and the whipped cream to create a fantastic dessert – and don't forget to top it all off with an ice cream cone. The only question is – do you want sprinkles?

Materials

HOOK SIZE: C

YARN: Mint green for ice cream

Dark brown for chocolate sauce

White for whipped cream

Red for cherry

Light brown for ice cream cone

A short wooden stick for support

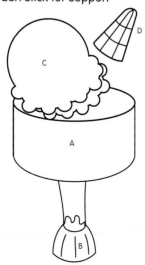

Structure

Part A: Sundae glass

Part B: Sundae glass base

Part C: Ice cream

Part D: Toppings

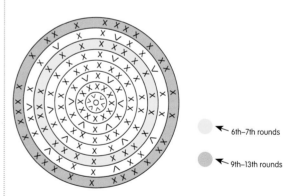

← 6th–7th rounds

← 9th–13th rounds

Sundae glass (part A)

Using brown yarn, make a loop with the tail end of the yarn on the right, keeping the ball end on the left.

Pull the ball end through the loop.

Make one ch through the loop on the hook you have drawn through to secure the circle.

Work 6sc into the circle and complete the circle with sl st into the first sc.

1st round: 2sc into each st. Change to mint green yarn.

2nd round: 1sc in all sts.

3rd round: *1sc, 2sc into next st. *6 times.

4th round: As round 2.

5th round: *5sc, 2sc into next st. *3 times.

6th–7th rounds: As round 2.

8th round: 1dc in each of next 2sc, *2sc in next sc, 1sc in next sc *10 times

9th–13th rounds: As round 2.

Fasten off.

Using the brown yarn, you need to make a disc to cover the top of the sundae glass. Make a circle to start, as for the sundae glass.

Work 6sc into the circle and complete the circle with sl st into the first sc.

1st round: 2sc into each 6sc.

2nd round: *1sc, 2sc into next st. *6 times.

3rd round: *2sc, 2sc into next st. *6 times.

4th round: *3sc, 2sc into next st. *6 times.

Continue working rounds, increasing in the same way, until the disc is big enough to cover the top of the sundae glass. Fasten off.

Sew the brown disc onto the glass, with some stuffing inside. It might be too floppy to stand by itself, so to make it more sturdy, put a wooden stick inside as you stuff.

Sundae glass base (part B)

Use white yarn.

Make a loop with the tail end of the yarn on the right, keeping the ball end on the left.

Pull the ball end through the loop.

Make one ch through the loop on the hook you have drawn through to secure the circle.

Work 6sc into the circle and complete the circle with sl st into the first sc.

1st round: 2sc into each st.

2nd round: *1sc, 2sc into next st *6 times.

3rd round: *2sc, 2sc into next st. *6 times.

4th round: 1sc in all sts.

5th round: *2sc, sc2tog. *6 times.

6th round: As round 4.

Fasten off.

Embroider long stitches around the base to look like the lines on a glass base.

Sew A and B together.

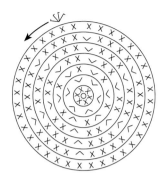

Ice cream (part C)

With mint green, make a loop with the tail end of the yarn on the right, keeping the ball end on the left.

Pull the ball end through the loop.

Make one ch through the loop on the hook you have drawn through to secure the circle.

Work 6sc into the circle and complete the circle with sl st into the first sc.

1st round: 2sc into each st.

2nd round: *1sc, 2sc into next st *6 times.

3rd round: *2sc, 2sc into next st. *6 times.

4th round: *3sc, 2sc into next st. *6 times.

5th round: *4sc, 2sc into next st. *6 times.

6th–10th rounds: 1sc in all sts.

11th round: 5hdc in all sts.

Fasten off.

This is for the main ice cream. If you want to add some layers of chocolate sauce, make a random number of dc into the same st and repeat, using brown or white yarn.

Ice cream cone (part D)

Using light brown, make a loop with the tail end of the yarn on the right, keeping the ball end on the left.

Pull the ball end through the loop.

Make one ch through the loop on the hook you have drawn through to secure the circle.

Work 6sc into the circle and complete the circle with sl st into the first sc.

1st round: *1sc, 2sc into next st. *3 times.

2nd–5th rounds: 1sc in all sts.

6th round: *1sc into each of next two sc, 2sc in next sc. *Repeat to end.

7th–9th round: 1sc in all sts.

Fasten off.

Add as many toppings as you like to your delicious ice cream sundae!

← 2th–5th rounds

← 7th–9th rounds

Chapter 3

Treats
from the
Cookie
Jar

Chocolate Chip Cookies

Probably everyone's favorite, who can resist a chocolate chip cookie (or three), washed down with an ice-cold glass of creamy milk? At least with these cookies, you won't be tempted to eat all the dough before they are baked!

Materials

HOOK SIZE: C

YARN: Light brown yarn for the cookie

Dark brown yarn for the chocolate chips

Cookie

With light brown yarn, make a loop with the tail end of the yarn on the right, keeping the ball end on the left.

Pull the ball end through the loop.

Make one ch through the loop on the hook you have drawn through to secure the circle.

6sc into the circle and complete the circle with sl st into the first sc.

1st round: 2sc into each st

2nd round: *1sc, 2sc into next st. *6 times.

3rd round: *2sc, 2sc into next st. *6 times.

4th round: *3sc, 2sc into next st. *6 times.

Fasten off.

Make two of these discs.

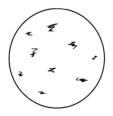

Chocolate chips

These are made by embroidering French knots onto the cookie.

Thread a tapestry needle with a length of dark brown yarn. Fasten the yarn to the underside of one cookie disc. Bring the needle out on the right side, where you want to make a chocolate chip. Holding the yarn tight and keeping the needle close to the place where the yarn comes out, wrap the yarn around the needle two or three times. Keeping the yarn tight, push the needle back into the cookie close to where the yarn came out. Pull the thread through to make a French knot.

Make as many French knots as you like for lots of chocolate chips.

Finishing up

Using light brown yarn, sew the two discs together, leaving a gap for stuffing.

Stuff and then sew the gap closed.

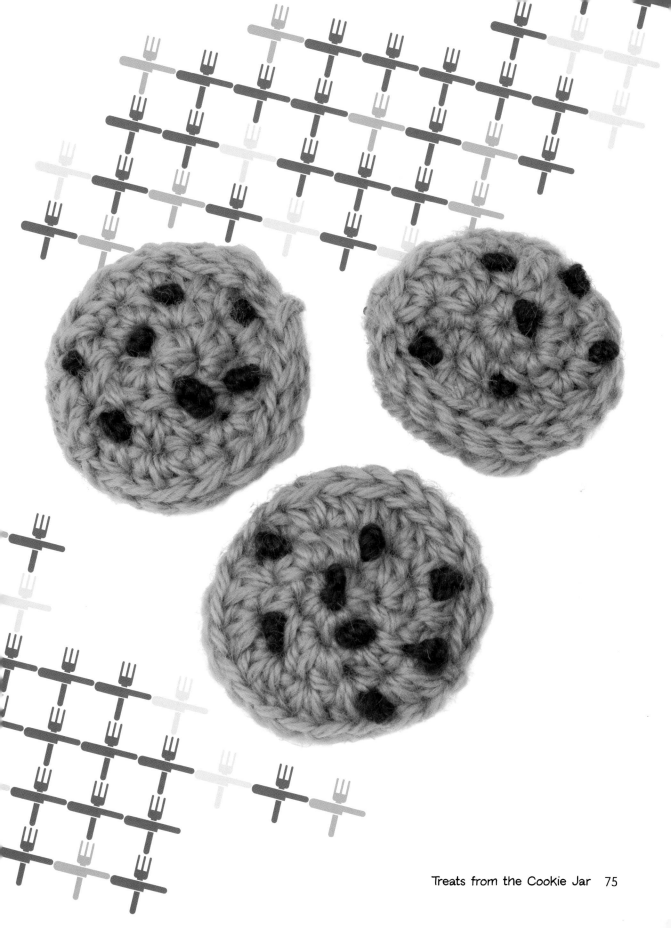

Go, Go Gingerbread Man!

"Run, run, as fast as you can. You can't catch me. I'm the Gingerbread Man!" Make sure this gingerbread man doesn't jump up off his baking tray and get away from you. The fox in the fairy tale might gobble him up, gumdrop buttons and all.

Materials

HOOK SIZE: C

YARN: Brown yarn for gingerbread man

White yarn for icing

Any colorful yarn for the gumdrop buttons

Black thread for eyes, red for a smiley mouth

Structure

The Gingerbread man is made up from six parts, with three different patterns.

Part A: Head

Part B: Body

Part C: Arms and legs

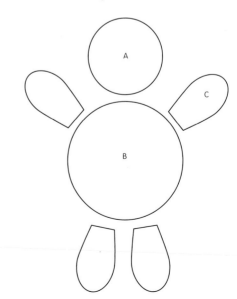

Head (part A)

With brown yarn, make a loop with the tail end of the yarn on the right, keeping the ball end on the left.

Pull the ball end through the loop.

Make one ch through the loop on the hook you have drawn through to secure the circle.

Work 6sc into the circle and complete the circle with sl st into the first sc.

1st round: 2sc into each st

2nd round: *1sc, 2sc into next st. *6 times.

3rd round: *2sc, 2sc into next st. *6 times.

4th round: *3sc, 2sc into next st. *6 times.

Fasten off.

Make 2 head pieces.

Body (part B)

With brown yarn, make a loop with the tail end of the yarn on the right, keeping the ball end on the left.

Pull the ball end through the loop.

Make one ch through the loop on the hook you have drawn through to secure the circle.

Work 6sc into the circle and complete the circle with sl st into the first sc.

1st round: 2sc into each st

2nd round: *1sc, 2sc into next st. *6 times.

3rd round: *2sc, 2sc into next st. *6 times.

4th round: *3sc, 2sc into next st. *6 times.

5th round: *4sc, 2sc into next st. *6 times.

6th round: *5sc, 2sc into next st. *6 times.

Fasten off.

Make 2 body pieces.

Arms and legs (part C)

With brown yarn, make a loop with the tail end of the yarn on the right, keeping the ball end on the left.

Pull the ball end through the loop.

Make one ch through the loop on the hook you have drawn through to secure the circle.

Work 6sc into the circle and complete the circle with sl st into the first sc.

1st round: 2sc into each st

2nd round: *1sc, 2sc into next st. *6 times.

3rd round: *2sc, 2sc into next st. *6 times.

4th round: 1sc in all sts.

Repeat round 4 until piece measures 1¼in.

Make 4 pieces.

Finishing up

Sew the two head pieces together, leaving a gap for stuffing. Stuff and sew up the gap. Repeat with the body pieces. Sew the head to the body. Stuff the arms and legs and sew to the body. Then chain stitch all around the outline in white yarn to make an iced edge.

Use chain stitch to add some gumdrop buttons and then embroider two eyes and a mouth.

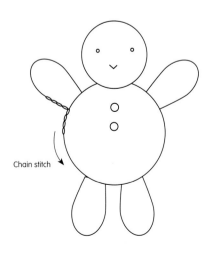

Chain stitch

For 1¼in (3cm)

Jam-tastic Treats

If there are any cookie hounds in your life, you can keep them happy with these jammy delights. Make up a big batch and hide them in the cookie jar.

Materials

HOOK SIZE: C

YARN: Light brown yarn for the cookie

Bright red yarn for jam

Front

With light brown yarn, make a loop with the tail end of the yarn on the right, keeping the ball end on the left.

Pull the ball end through the loop.

Make one ch through the loop on the hook you have drawn through to secure the circle.

Work 6sc into the circle and complete the circle with sl st into the first sc. Ch2 to start the next round.

1st round: ch2, 1hdc, *2hdc into each st. *5 times

2nd round: ch2, 2hdc around the stem of next st on the row below, from the front of the work, *1hdc, 2hdc around the stem of next st on the row below, from the front of the work. *5 times.

Fasten off.

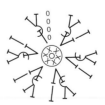

Back

With light brown yarn, make a loop with the tail end of the yarn on the right, keeping the ball end on the left.

Pull the ball end through the loop.

Make one ch through the loop on the hook you have drawn through to secure the circle.

Work 6sc into the circle and complete the circle with sl st into the first sc.

1st round: 2sc into each st

2nd round: *1sc, 2sc into next st. *6 times.

3rd round: *2sc, 2sc into next st. *6 times.

4th round: *3sc, 2sc into next st. *6 times.

Fasten off.

Jam

With bright red yarn, make a loop with the tail end of the yarn on the right, keeping the ball end on the left.

Pull the ball end through the loop.

Make one ch through the loop on the hook you have drawn through to secure the circle.

Work 6sc into the circle and complete the circle with sl st into the first sc.

1st round: 2sc into each st

2nd round: *1sc, 2sc into next st. *6 times..

Fasten off.

Finishing up

Sew the jam onto the front part of the cookie. Then sew the front and back parts together.

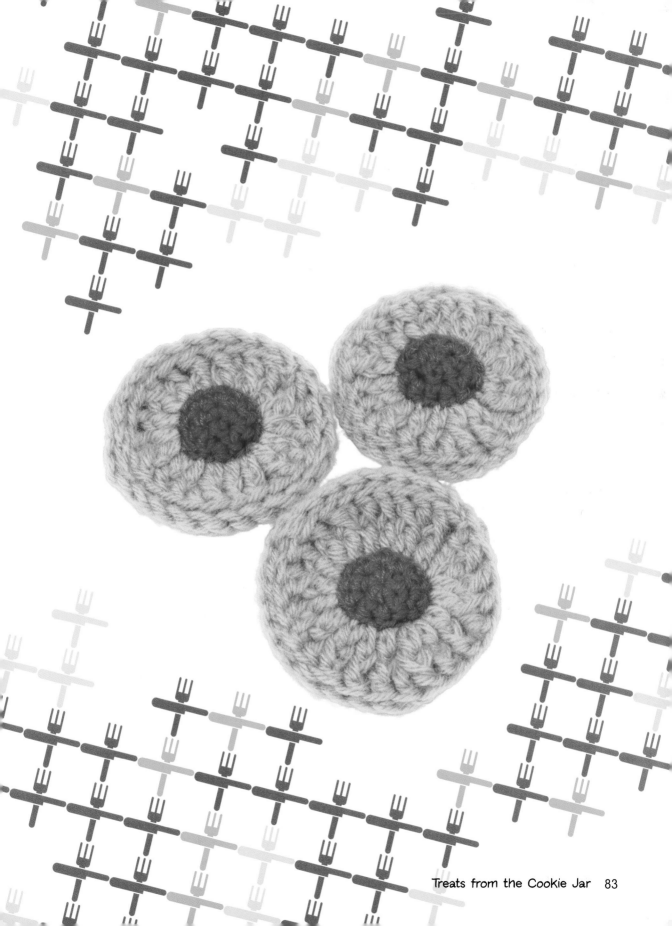

Buttery Butter Cookies

When you're setting up a traditional tea party, only the best will do – the finest china, some Earl Grey tea, and the poshest treats you can make. Try your hand at these refined butter cookies and you won't fail to impress.

Materials

HOOK SIZE: C

YARN: Light brown

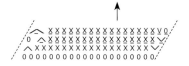

Using light brown yarn, ch20; turn.

1st row: ch1, 2sc into first st, work sc to last 2sts, sc2tog, turn.

2nd row: ch1, (working into back loop) sc2tog, work sc to last st, 2sc into last st, turn.

Repeat rows 1 and 2 until the work measures 6in. Working into the back loops of stitches will give a ridged effect to the finished piece.

Fasten off.

Finishing up

If the finished edge is A and the beginning edge is B, bring A and B together to make a seam. Sew along the seam to form a cylinder shape.

Using a length of yarn and a tapestry needle, run a few stitches around the top and bottom of the cylinder and then pull on the yarn to gather up the ends and twist into a "whirl" shape. Secure the ends of the yarn.

If you think the cookie needs a bit of stuffing, add this just before you gather up the ends.

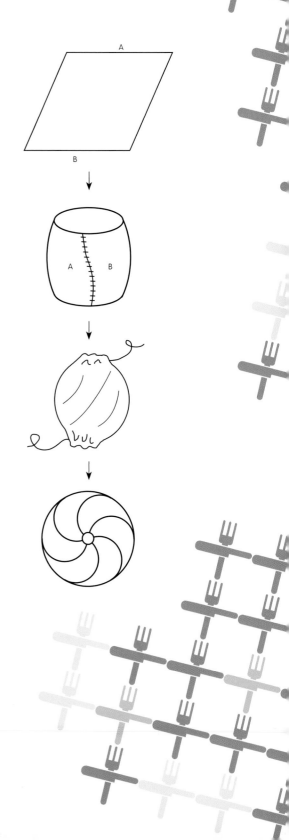

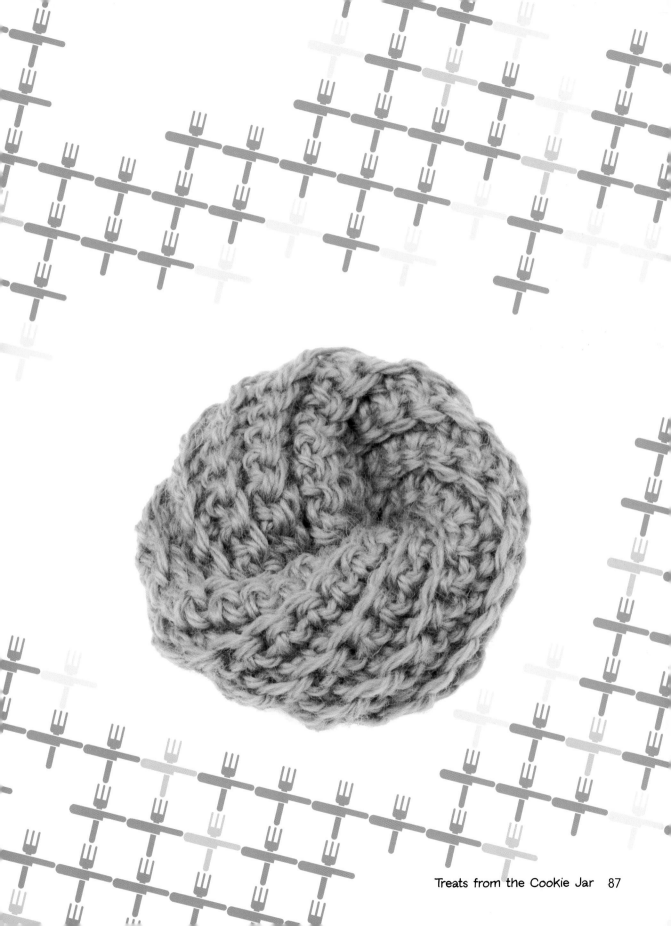

Special Fortune Cookies

Who knows what the future holds? Make up some crazy predictions and slip them inside these fun fortune cookies and give your friends and loved ones a laugh.

Materials

HOOK SIZE: C

YARN: Light brown yarn

Small rectangles of white cotton to make fortune-telling "paper"

Fabric marker for writing fortunes (optional)

Using light brown yarn, make a loop with the tail end of the yarn on the right, keeping the ball end on the left.

Pull the ball end through the loop.

Make one ch through the loop on the hook you have drawn through to secure the circle.

Work 6sc into the circle and complete the circle with sl st into the first sc.

1st round: 2sc into each st

2nd round: *1sc, 2sc into next st. *6 times.

3rd round: *2sc, 2sc into next st. *6 times.

4th round: *3sc, 2sc into next st. *6 times.

5th round: *4sc, 2sc into next st. *6 times.

6th round: *5sc, 2sc into next st. *6 times.

Fasten off.

Make as many as you want.

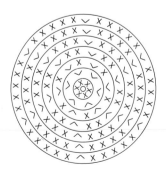

Finishing up

If you want to have some fun, write silly predictions on the rectangles of white cotton. When your friends pick up their fortune cookies they can have a laugh.

Use a fabric marker and write on just one end of the fabric – the pieces are folded in half and sewn into the cookies.

Fold the cookie disc in half. Stuff it, insert a piece of folded fabric in between the seam and sew around the edge.

To make it look like a typical fortune cookie, make a stitch in the straight edge and then pass the needle and yarn through to the curved edge. Pull the yarn tight – this will make a fold in the straight edge – and secure the yarn to hold it in place.

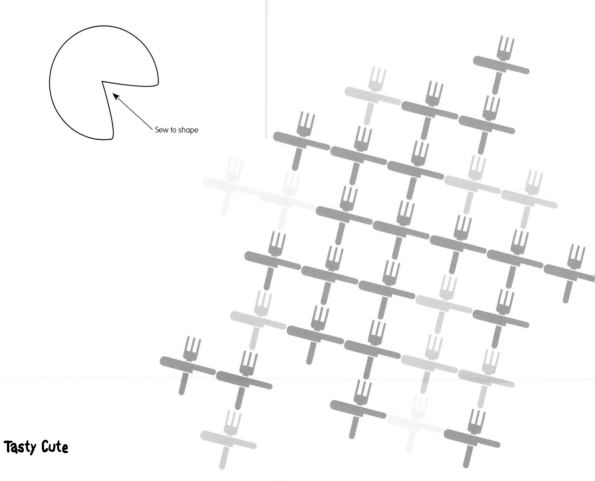

Sew to shape

Chapter 4

The Sweetest Little Candies

PÂTISSERIE FINE

PÂTISSERIE FINE

Keep it Sweet Candies

You can create your own candy heaven with these bright and colorful candies. You won't want to keep these striped treats hidden in a tin. Remember, the best candies are the ones that last forever!

Materials

HOOK SIZE: C

YARN: Any color of yarn will work for the wrapped candies; you can make them as colorful as you like! Use two different color yarns for each to make them striped.

Pink yarn for the strawberry candies.

Wrapped candies

The structure of each wrapped candy is very simple. All you need to make is a colorful rectangle which is then twisted into a pretty bow shape! Just like the real thing!

Using your first chosen color, ch16; turn.

1st row: 1sc in 3rd ch from hook, 14sc, turn.

2nd row: Change to second color, ch1, 14sc, turn.

Repeat row 2 until 12 rows in total have been worked, alternating colors through the rows.

Fasten off.

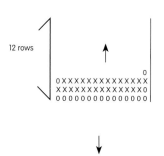

Finishing up

Lay out the rectangle you've just made and put a ball of stuffing in the middle. Wrap the rectangle around the stuffing and twist the ends closed – just like a real sweetie. Secure with a few sewing stitches.

Strawberry candy

Using pink yarn, make a loop with the tail end of the yarn on the right, keeping the ball end on the left.

Pull the ball end through the loop.

Make one ch through the loop on the hook you have drawn through to secure the circle.

Work 6sc into the circle and complete the circle with sl st into the first sc.

1st round: 3sc into the first st, 2sc into next st, 1sc into next st, 3sc into next st, 1sc into next st, 2sc into last st.

2nd round: 3sc into each of next 3 sts, 3sc, 3sc into each of next 3 sts, 3sc.

3rd–6th rounds: 1sc in all sts.

Fasten off.

This makes the top of the candy. To make the base, work rounds 1 and 2 as above; fasten off.

Put a bit off stuffing into the top part of the candy and then sew the two parts together.

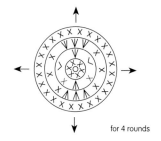

for 4 rounds

Candy top

Candy base

Teeny-tiny Truffles

For that perfect present for a special someone, nothing beats a beautiful box of gorgeous chocolates. These hand-made goodies would melt anyone's soft center. Make them for your beloved and they'll have a sweet treat to keep forever.

Materials

HOOK SIZE: C

YARN: Dark brown yarn for coffee truffle and almond praline

Light brown yarn for the almond

White yarn for the white chocolate truffle

Light brown textured yarn to decorate the coffee truffle

Dark and mid-brown embroidery thread to decorate the white chocolate truffle and the almond praline

Coffee truffle

Using dark brown yarn, make a loop with the tail end of the yarn on the right, keeping the ball end on the left.

Pull the ball end through the loop.

Make one ch through the loop on the hook you have drawn through to secure the circle.

Work 6sc into the circle and complete the circle with sl st into the first sc.

1st round: 2sc into each st

2nd round: *1sc, 2sc into next st. *6 times.

3rd round: *2sc, 2sc into next st. *6 times.

4th–7th rounds: 1sc in all sts.

8th round: *2sc, sc2tog. *6 times.

9th round: *1sc, sc2tog. *6 times.

10th round: *sc2tog. *6 times.

Fasten off.

Use light brown textured yarn to embroider on icing lines. Add some stuffing and sew the opening closed.

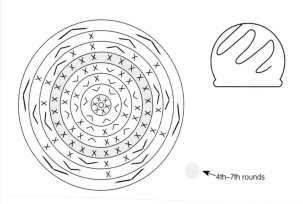

4th–7th rounds

Far right: White chocolate truffle
Bottom right: Almond praline
Near right: Coffee truffle

White chocolate truffle

With white yarn, make a loop with the tail end of the yarn on the right, keeping the ball end on the left.

Pull the ball end through the loop.

Make one ch through the loop on the hook you have drawn through to secure the circle.

Work 6sc into the circle and complete the circle with sl st into the first sc.

1st round: 2sc into each st

2nd round: *1sc, 2sc into next st. *6 times.

3rd round: *2sc, 2sc into next st. *6 times.

4th–7th rounds: 1sc in all sts.

Fasten off.

This makes the top of the truffle. To make the base, work rounds 1 to 3 as above; fasten off.

Using chain stitch embroider some chocolate decoration on the top section with dark brown thread.

Put a bit off stuffing into the top part of the truffle and then sew the two parts together.

4th–7th rounds

Almond praline

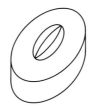
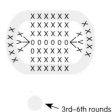

3rd–6th rounds

Using dark brown yarn, make ch7.

1st round: 1sc in 2nd ch from hook, 4sc, 3sc into the end of foundation ch, along other side of chain 6sc, 3sc into 6th ch of foundation ch.

2nd round: 7sc, 2sc into next st, 8sc, 2sc into next st, 1sc.

3rd–6th rounds: 1sc in all sts.

Fasten off.

This makes the top of the praline. To make the base, work rounds 1 and 2 as above; fasten off.

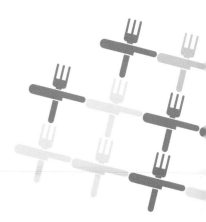

Almond

Using light brown yarn, make a loop with the tail end of the yarn on the right, keeping the ball end on the left.

Pull the ball end through the loop.

Make one ch through the loop on the hook you have drawn through to secure the circle.

Work 6sc into the circle and complete the circle with sl st into the first sc.

1st round: 2sc into each st

2nd–5th rounds: 1sc in all sts.

6th round: sc2tog in all sts.

7th round: 1sc in all sts.

Fasten off.

Using mid-brown thread, embroider some lines over the almond. Put a little stuffing into the almond and sew it to the almond-praline top. Stuff the top part of the almond praline then sew on the base.

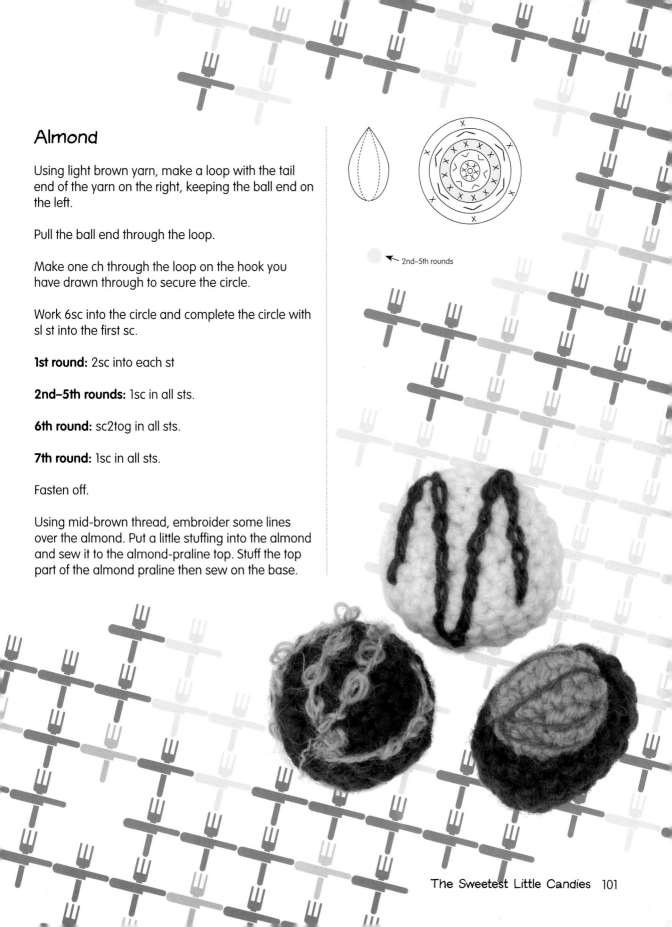

← 2nd–5th rounds

Little Licorice

These licorice candies are always a pretty and popular choice. Make lots and lots in bright colors and fill your candy jar to the brim.

Materials

HOOK SIZE: C

YARN: Black yarn for all the bonbons

Pink yarn for the pink licorice

Yellow yarn for yellow licorice

White yarn for the licorice sandwich

Pink licorice

Using black yarn, make a loop with the tail end of the yarn on the right, keeping the ball end on the left.

Pull the ball end through the loop.

Make one ch through the loop on the hook you have drawn through to secure the circle.

Work 6sc into the circle and complete the circle with sl st into the first sc.

1st round: 2sc into each st

2nd–5th rounds: Change to pink yarn, 1sc in all sts.

6th round: Change to black yarn, sc2tog in all sts.

Fasten off.

Add some stuffing and then sew the opening closed.

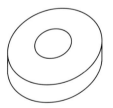

←2nd–5th rounds

Far top right: Yellow licorice
Bottom right: Licorice sandwich
Top right: Pink licorice

Yellow licorice

Using black yarn, make a loop with the tail end of the yarn on the right, keeping the ball end on the left.

Pull the ball end through the loop.

Make one ch through the loop on the hook you have drawn through to secure the circle.

Work 6sc into the circle and complete the circle with sl st into the first sc.

1st round: Change to yellow yarn, 1sc in all sts.

Repeat 1st round until work measures 1½in.

Next round: Change to black yarn, sc2tog in all sts.

Fasten off.

Stuff the cylinder shape you've just made and then close with a few stitches.

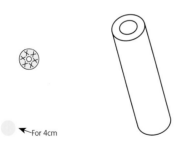

←For 4cm

Licorice sandwich

Using black, ch9; turn

1st row: 1sc in 3rd ch from hook, sc to end, turn.

2nd row: ch1, sc to end, turn.

Repeat 2nd row until the work measures 1½in. Make two more rectangles the same size but in white yarn.

Fold each rectangle in half and secure with a few stitches around the edge.

Sandwich your black piece between the two white ones and sew together.

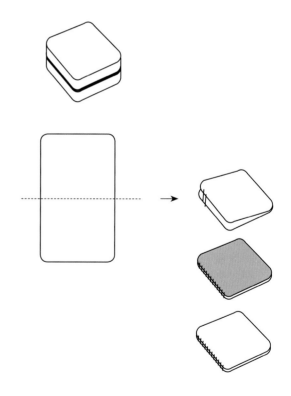

Finest French Macaroons

Pale and pretty, light and fluffy, macaroons are ideal girly gifts. Make a box of these fancy French confections and share the sweetness with your friends at the next party.

Materials

HOOK SIZE: C

YARN: An assortment of pastel-colored yarn

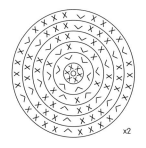

Using your chosen color, make a loop with the tail end of the yarn on the right, keeping the ball end on the left.

Pull the ball end through the loop.

Make one ch through the loop on the hook you have drawn through to secure the circle.

Work 6sc into the circle and complete the circle with sl st into the first sc.

1st round: 2sc into each st

2nd round: *1sc, 2sc into next st. *6 times.

3rd round: *2sc, 2sc into next st. *6 times.

4th round: *3sc, 2sc into next st. *6 times.

5th round: *4sc, 2sc into next st. *6 times.

Fasten off.

Make another in the same color.

Finishing up

Sew the two circles together, leaving a small gap for the stuffing. Stuff and then sew the gap closed.

Using the same or a different color, chain stitch around the seam to make the filling!

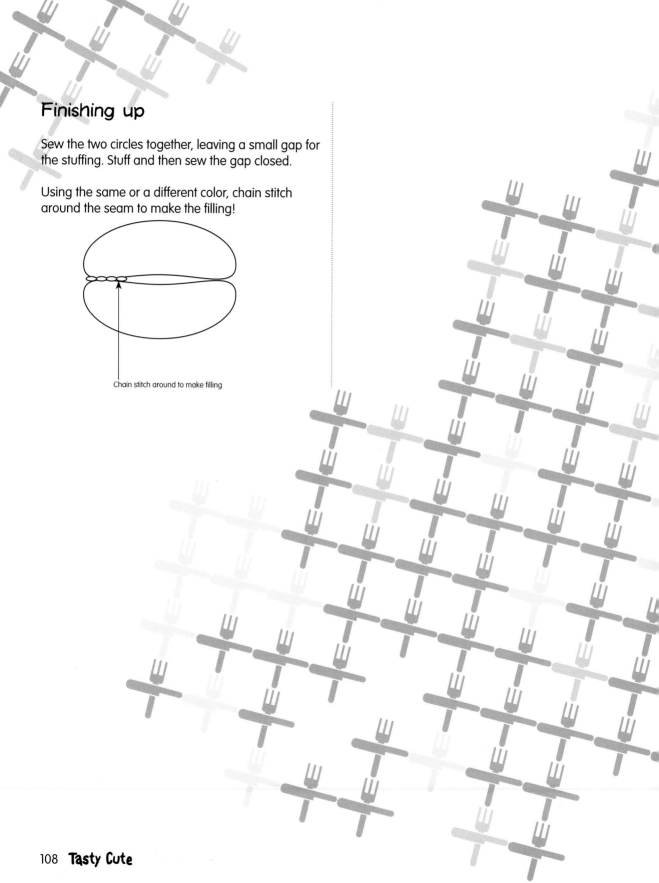

Chain stitch around to make filling

Lovely Lollipop

All kids love a lollipop to lick. Recreate this childhood favorite and take a trip down Memory Lane. Only this time, you don't have to worry about blowing all your pocket money at once.

Materials

HOOK SIZE: C

YARN: Red and white for lollipop

Brown for stick

Plus a short wooden stick, about 6in long, for support

The lollipop is made from one piece that is shaped like a striped diamond.

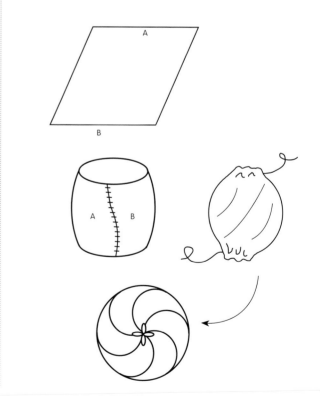

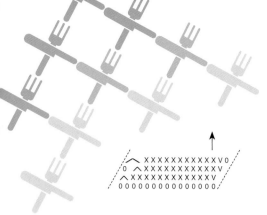

Using white yarn, ch15; turn.

1st row: 2sc into first st, work sc to last 2 sts, sc2tog, turn.

2nd row: sc2tog, work sc to last st, 2sc into last st, turn.

Repeat rows 1 and 2 until work measures 8in, changing color every 2 rows.

Fasten off.

If the finished edge is A and the beginning edge is B, bring A and B together to make a seam. Sew along the seam to form a cylinder shape.

Using a length of yarn and a tapestry needle, run a few stitches around the top and bottom of the cylinder and then pull on the yarn to gather up the ends and twist into a swirly shape. Flatten into a disc and make a stitch through the center to secure.

Now you can see the shape of the lollipop!

Lolly stick

Using brown, ch5; turn

1st row: 1sc in 2nd ch from hook, sc to end, turn.

2nd row: ch1, 3sc, turn.

Repeat 2nd row until the work measures about 6in.

Fold it in half lengthwise and sew along one short side and along the length. You can slip a small wooden stick inside to give support if you like.

Stitch the stick onto your lollipop.

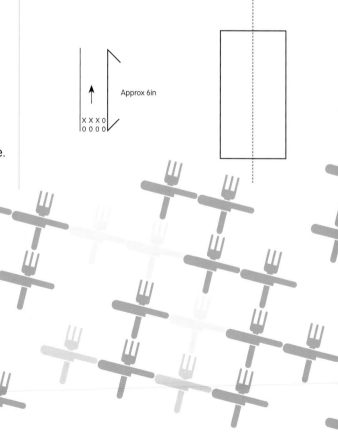

Approx 6in

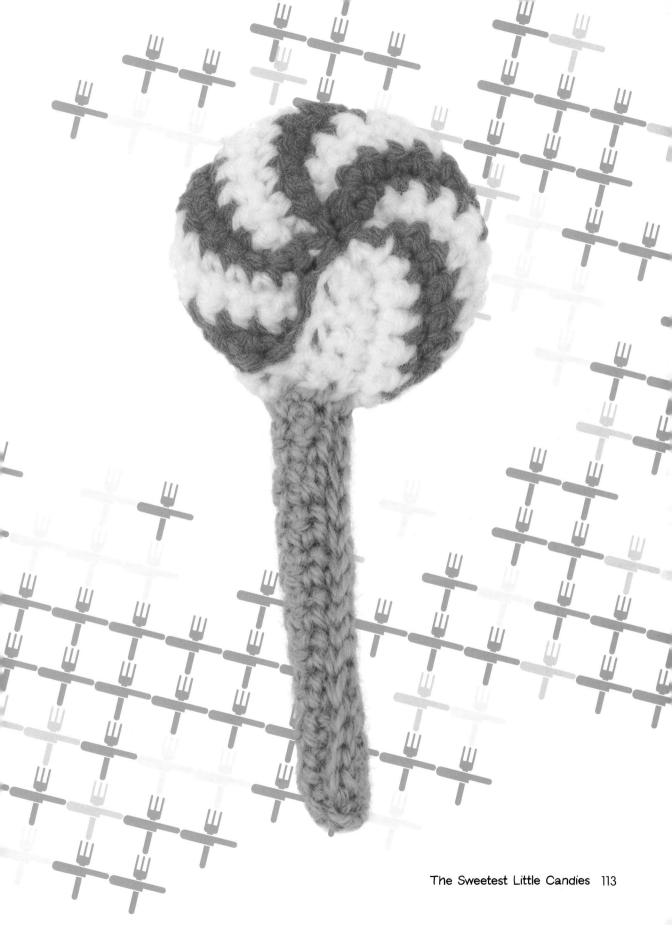

Chapter 5

The
Healthy
Option

Gourmet Garden Salad

Get creative with the crochet and mix up some of your salad favorites. Combine different leaves with thick slices of tomato, stir in some button mushrooms, onions, anchovies, and boiled egg, and there you have it – a salad that stays forever fresh!

Materials

HOOK SIZE: C

YARN: Different shades of green for lettuce

White yarn and yellow yarn for the egg

Red yarn for tomato slices

Brown Lurex yarn and purple yarn for anchovies

White yarn for onion slices and mushrooms

Salad leaves

Using a green yarn, ch9; turn

1st round: 1sc into third ch from hook, 1sc into each of next ch5, 3sc in final ch, work along other side of ch 1sc into each of next ch2, 3hdc into each of next ch3, 3dc into each of next 2 sts.

2nd round: 3dc into each of next 3 sts, 3hdc into next st, 1sc into each st to first 3hdc, 3hdc into each st to the same point, working all around the piece, sl st to first hdc.

Fasten off.

Use different shades of green to make lots of leaves. Use ch9 to start for smaller leaves, and ch13 to start larger leaves.

Onion

With white yarn, ch12. Join with a sl st to first ch to make a circle.

1st round: 1sc in all sts, finishing with sl st to first st.

Fasten off.

Make as many as you like. You can start with any number of chains to make a smaller or bigger onion ring.

Tomato slice

With red yarn, ch6. Join with a sl st to first ch to make a circle.

1st round: 12sc into circle.

2nd round: 6sc, 1dc into 1st sc, *ch2, skip next sc, 1dc into next sc. *5 times. Join with a sl st to 3rd ch of ch6.

Fasten off.

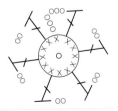

Anchovy

With purple yarn, ch9.

1st row: 1sc into third ch from hook, 1sc into each st to end, turn.

2nd row: change to Lurex yarn, sc2tog, 1sc into each st to end.

Fasten off.

```
∧ X X X X o
X X X X X X o
o o o o o o o
```

Egg

With yellow yarn, make a loop with the tail end of the yarn on the right, keeping the ball end on the left.

Pull the ball end through the loop.

Make one ch through the loop on the hook you have drawn through to secure the circle.

6sc into the circle and complete the circle with sl st into the first sc.

1st round: 2sc into each st

2nd round: *1sc, 2sc into next st. *6 times.

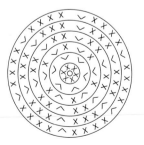

3rd round: Change to white yarn. *2sc, 2sc into next st. *6 times.

4th round: *3sc, 2sc into next st. *6 times.

5th round: *4sc, 2sc into next st. *6 times.

Fasten off.

Fold the circle in half and sew around the edge, leaving a gap for stuffing. Stuff and then sew the gap closed.

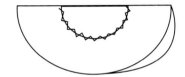

Mushroom

With white yarn, make a loop with the tail end of the yarn on the right, keeping the ball end on the left.

Pull the ball end through the loop.

Make one ch through the loop on the hook you have drawn through to secure the circle.

6sc into the circle and complete the circle with sl st into the first sc.

1st round: 2sc into each st

2nd round: *1sc, 2sc into next st. *6 times.

3rd round: *2sc, 2sc into next st. *6 times.

4th–6th rounds: 1sc in all sts.

Fasten off.

This makes the top of the mushroom.

To make the stem, work as for the mushroom top up to round 2. Then work rounds of all sc until the stem is long enough.

Stuff the top and the stem and then stitch together.

Make as many tasty salad ingredients as you like!

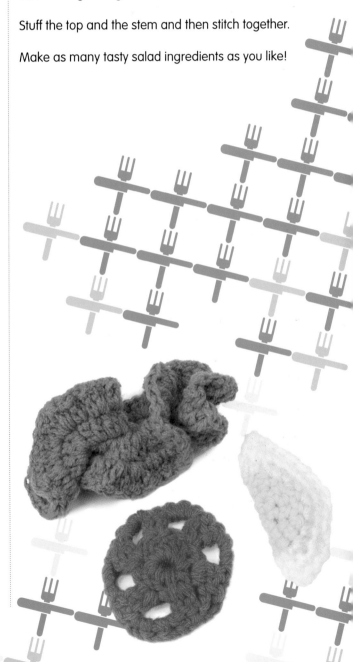

Perfect Pear

Next time you're filling the fruit bowl, pop in one of these pears and see if anyone notices the difference. Just make sure you let everyone in on the secret before they try to take a bite!

Materials

HOOK SIZE: C

YARN: Green yarn for the pear body

Dark brown yarn for stem

Mid-brown yarn for markings

← 4th-9th rounds

Pear body

With green yarn, make a loop with the tail end of the yarn on the right, keeping the ball end on the left.

Pull the ball end through the loop.

Make one ch through the loop on the hook you have drawn through to secure the circle.

Work 6sc into the circle and complete the circle with sl st into the first sc.

1st round: 2sc into each st

2nd round: *1sc, 2sc into next st. *6 times.

3rd round: *2sc, 2sc into next st. *6 times.

4th–9th rounds: 1sc in all sts.

10th round: *4sc, sc2tog. *4 times.

11th round: *3sc, sc2tog. *4 times.

12th round: *2sc, sc2tog. *4 times.

13th round: *sc2tog. *6 times.

Fasten off.

Fill with stuffing and then stitch opening closed.

Pear stem

With brown yarn, ch6.

1st row: 1sc in 2nd ch from hook, sc to end.

Fasten off.

Sew the stem on to the top of the pear. With mid-brown yarn, embroider a few markings on to the pear body.

```
X X X X O
O O O O O
```

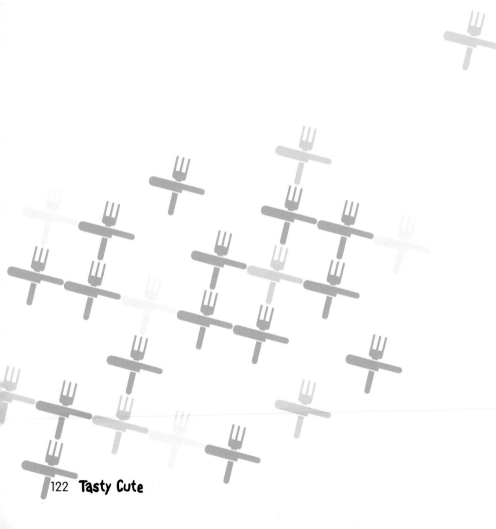

Peas in a Pod

We all need to give peas a chance! So why don't you make these three lovely little legumes? Nestled in their cozy pod, these cute crocheted vegetables are just bursting with green goodness. They're as perfect as... well, peas in a pod!

Materials

HOOK SIZE: C

YARN: Dark pea-green yarn for peas

Light green yarn for pea pod

Pod

With light green yarn, 10ch.

1st round: 1sc into 3rd ch from hook, 7sc, 3sc into the end ch of foundation chain, 9sc worked into unused side of foundation chain, 3sc in same place as last st.

2nd round: 9sc, 2sc into each of next 3sc, 9sc, 2sc into each of next 3sc.

3rd round: 9sc, *2sc into next sc, 1sc, *3 times, 9sc, *2sc into next sc, 1sc, *3 times.

4th round: 9sc, *2sc into next sc, 2sc, *3 times, 9sc, *2sc into next sc, 2sc, *3 times.

5th round: sc in all sts.

Fasten off.

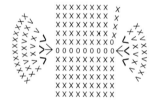

Pinch both ends of the shape and slightly fold the edges in to make the pod; secure with a few stitches.

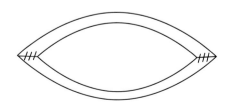

Pea

With dark pea-green yarn, make a loop with the tail end of the yarn on the right, keeping the ball end on the left.

Pull the ball end through the loop.

Make one ch through the loop on the hook you have drawn through to secure the circle.

Work 6sc into the circle and complete the circle with sl st into the first sc.

1st round: 2sc into each st

2nd round: *1sc, 2sc into next st. *6 times.

3rd–5th rounds: 1sc in all sts.

6th round: *1sc, sc2tog. *4 times.

7th round: *sc2tog. *4 times.

Fasten off.

Make 2 more exactly the same.

Stuff each pea and then sew the opening closed on each one.

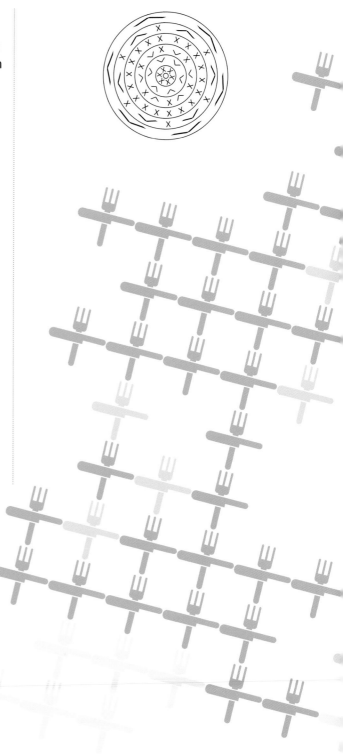

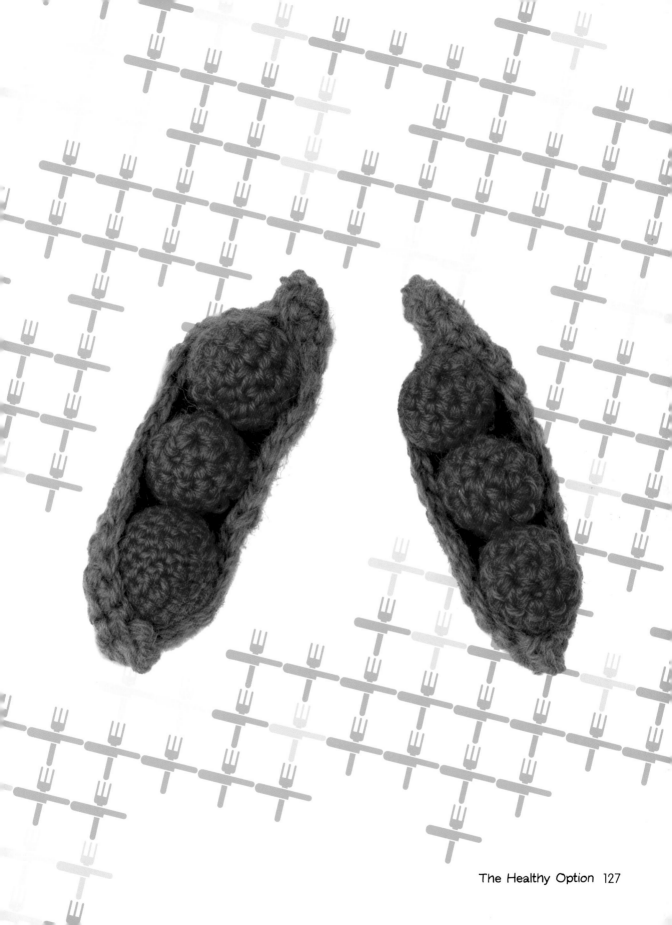

Go Bananas

Pack this banana in your lunchbox or picnic basket and no one will know that you have been playing with your food. And at least with this banana, there's no danger of anyone slipping on the peel!

Materials

HOOK SIZE: C

YARN: Banana-yellow yarn

Brown yarn for sugar spots

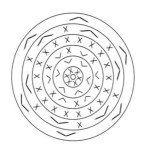

With yellow yarn, make a loop with the tail end of the yarn on the right, keeping the ball end on the left.

Pull the ball end through the loop.

Make one ch through the loop on the hook you have drawn through to secure the circle.

Work 6sc into the circle and complete the circle with sl st into the first sc.

1st round: 2sc into each st

2nd round: *1sc, 2sc into next st. *6 times.

3rd round: 1sc in all sts.

Repeat round 3 for 4¾in.

Next round: *1sc, sc2tog. *6 times.

Next round: *sc2tog. *6 times.

Change to brown yarn and work 2 rounds in sc.

Fasten off.

Finishing up

Using yellow yarn, chain stitch lines down the banana to make it look ribbed. Add a few brown spots with brown yarn.

Push stuffing into the banana and then sew the end opening closed.

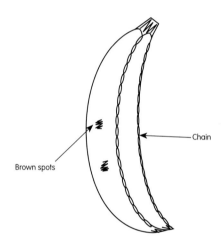

Brown spots

Chain

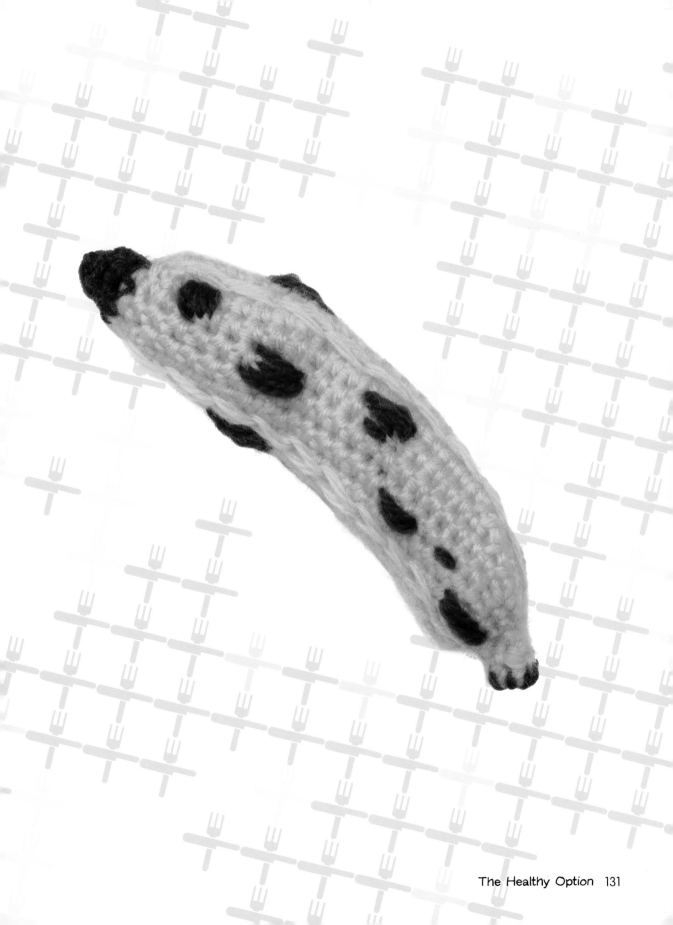

Fancy Fruit Tart

This fruit-i-licious tart is filled with sweet delights. Orange, kiwi, strawberry, and apple are packed into a perfect pastry tart. Make some next time you have a dinner party and your guests will have a dessert they can keep forever!

Materials

HOOK SIZE: C

YARN: Brown yarn for tart base

White yarn to mix with brown yarn for fondant filling

Fresh green yarn, dark brown yarn, and white yarn for kiwi

White yarn and bright red yarn for apple slices

Red yarn and dark green yarn for strawberries

Light green thread to embroider strawberry seeds

Orange yarn for orange slices

Structure

The base of the tart is made up from two parts:

Part A is the ribbed edge around the tart.

Part B is the bottom of the tart.

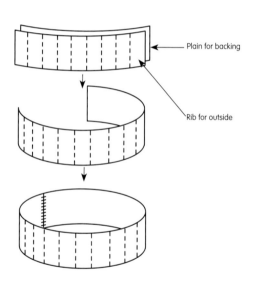

Plain for backing

Rib for outside

Edge of tart (Part A)

This is made in two parts. The outer part is a long rectangular piece that's been given a ribbed texture by working half double crochet stitches around the stem of the stitch on the row below.

The inner part is a rectangle the same size as the outer, that acts as a backing and makes the finished edge stiffer.

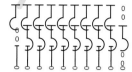

With the brown yarn, ch12; turn.

1st row: 1hdc into 4th ch from hook, hdc to end, turn.

2nd row: ch2, *1hdc around the stem of next st on the row below, from the front of the work. *Repeat to end, turn.

3rd row: ch2, *1hdc around the stem of next st on the row below, from the back of the work. *Repeat to end, turn.

Repeat 2nd and 3rd rows until it's long enough to make a good-sized tart.

Using the same yarn, make another piece exactly the same size and shape. You can work in either sc or dc instead of hdc. This piece forms the backing to make the edge of the tart stiffer.

Put the two pieces together and sew along the long sides. Curve into a ring and sew the short ends together.

Bottom of tart (Part B)

With the same brown yarn as the edge of tart, make a loop with the tail end of the yarn on the right, keeping the ball end on the left.

Pull the ball end through the loop.

Make one ch through the loop on the hook you have drawn through to secure the circle.

Work 6sc into the circle and complete the circle with sl st into the first sc.

1st round: 2sc into each st.

2nd round: *1sc, 2sc into next st. *6 times.

3rd round: *2sc, 2sc into next st. *6 times.

4th round: *3sc, 2sc into next st. *6 times.

Continue making a circle in the same way, adding 1sc between increases on each round. When the circle is big enough to fit the tart edge you made, fasten off.

Sew the bottom to the tart edge.

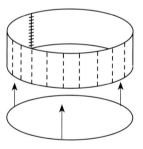

Now you have a cylinder-shaped tart base.

Just as you would need for an edible tart, we shall need some cream to fill the bottom of the tart.

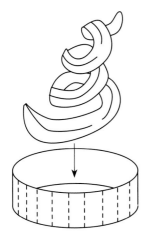

x2

Kiwi

With white yarn, make a loop with the tail end of the yarn on the right, keeping the ball end on the left.

Pull the ball end through the loop.

Make one ch through the loop on the hook you have drawn through to secure the circle.

Work 6sc into the circle and complete the circle with sl st into the first sc.

1st round: 2sc into each st.

2nd round: Change to brown yarn. *1sc, 2sc into next st. *6 times.

3rd round: Change to fresh green yarn. *2sc, 2sc into next st. *6 times.

Fasten off.

Make another piece the same, then sew the two together.

Fondant filling

The filling can be made with any color yarn. Here, a strand of brown and a strand of white yarn are used together.

The filling is made by a long piece of crochet, curled up in the tart. Start by making the chain as long as you need to fill your tart (it might need to be at least 12in.

1st row: 1hdc into 3rd ch from hook, hdc to end, turn.

2nd row: ch2, *1hdc around the stem of next st on the row below, from the front of the work. *Repeat to end.

Fasten off.

Curl the strip of cream into the bottom of the tart and stitch in place.

Now it's time to top your tart with some fresh fruit.

Orange segments

Using orange yarn, form a circle by wrapping the yarn around your finger, then insert the hook and make ch3.

1st round: 15dc into the circle. Join with sl st to top of ch3.

2nd round: ch3 *1dc around the stem of next st on the row below, from the front of the work, 2dc around the stem of next st on the row below, from the front of the work. *Repeat to end of round.

Fasten off.

Fold the circle in half and push some stuffing inside. Sew around the edges.

Apple slices

With white yarn, make a loop with the tail end of the yarn on the right, keeping the ball end on the left.

Pull the ball end through the loop.

Make one ch through the loop on the hook you have drawn through to secure the circle.

Work 6sc into the circle and complete the circle with sl st into the first sc.

1st round: 2sc into each st

2nd round: *1sc, 2sc into next st. *6 times.

3rd round: *2sc, 2sc into next st. *6 times.

4th round: *3sc, 2sc into next st. *6 times.

5th round: *4sc, 2sc into next st. *6 times.

6th round: Change to bright red yarn. *5sc, 2sc into next st. *6 times.

Fasten off.

Fold the circle in half and push some stuffing inside. Sew around the edges.

Strawberry

With red yarn, make a loop with the tail end of the yarn on the right, keeping the ball end on the left.

Pull the ball end through the loop.

Make one ch through the loop on the hook you have drawn through to secure the circle.

Work 5sc into the circle and complete the circle with sl st into the first sc.

1st round: 1sc into each 5sc.

2nd round: 2sc into each of 5sc.

3rd round: *1sc, 2sc into next st. *5 times.

4th–5th rounds: 1sc in all sts.

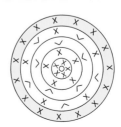

←4th–5th rounds

Fasten off.

Use light green thread to embroider little seeds on the outside. Stuff the strawberry and then sew the opening closed.

Strawberry top

With green yarn, ch6; turn.

1st row: 1sc into the third ch from the hook, sc to end.

Fasten off.

Make 5 little leaves like this and then stitch onto the top of your juicy strawberry.

Make as many of the different fruits as will fill your tart base!

```
X X X X 0
0 0 0 0 0   x5
```

Tasty Index

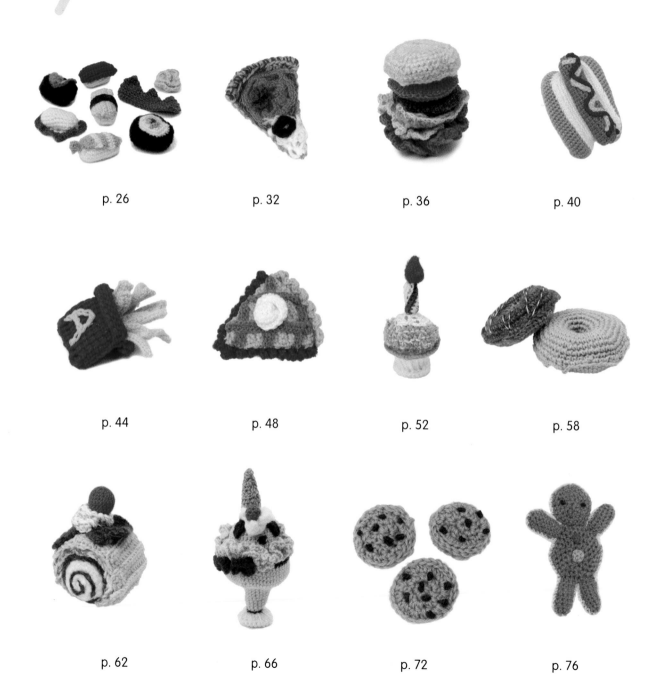

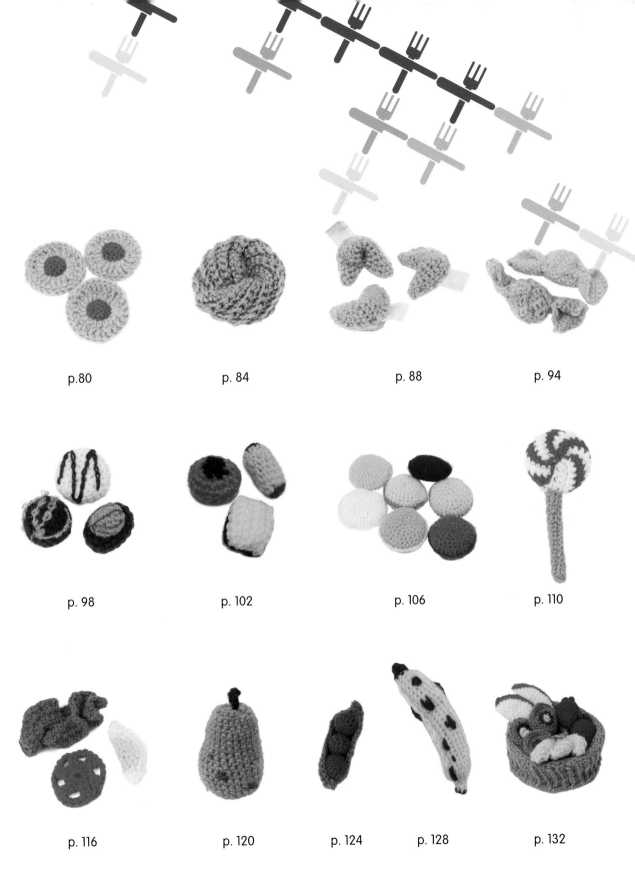

p.80

p. 84

p. 88

p. 94

p. 98

p. 102

p. 106

p. 110

p. 116

p. 120

p. 124

p. 128

p. 132

Resources

Enter the tasty-cute world of amigurumi. The following tried and tested retailers and suppliers can help you on your mission to fill your life with cuteness.

Yarns

Blue Sky Alpacas, Inc.

P.O. Box 88

Cedar, MN 55011

www.blueskyalpacas.com

Brown Sheep Yarn Company

10062 County Road

Mitchell, NE 69357

www.brownsheep.com

Knitting Fever, Inc.

www.knittingfever.com

Knitty City

208 W. 79th St.

New York, NY 10024

www.knittycity.com

Lion Brand Yarns

135 Kero Road

Carlstadt, NJ 07072

www.lionbrand.com

Misti Alpaca

P.O.Box 2532

Glen Ellyn, Illinois 60138

www.mistialpaca.com

Patons

320 Livingstone Avenue South

Listowel, ON N4W 3H3

www.patonsyarns.com

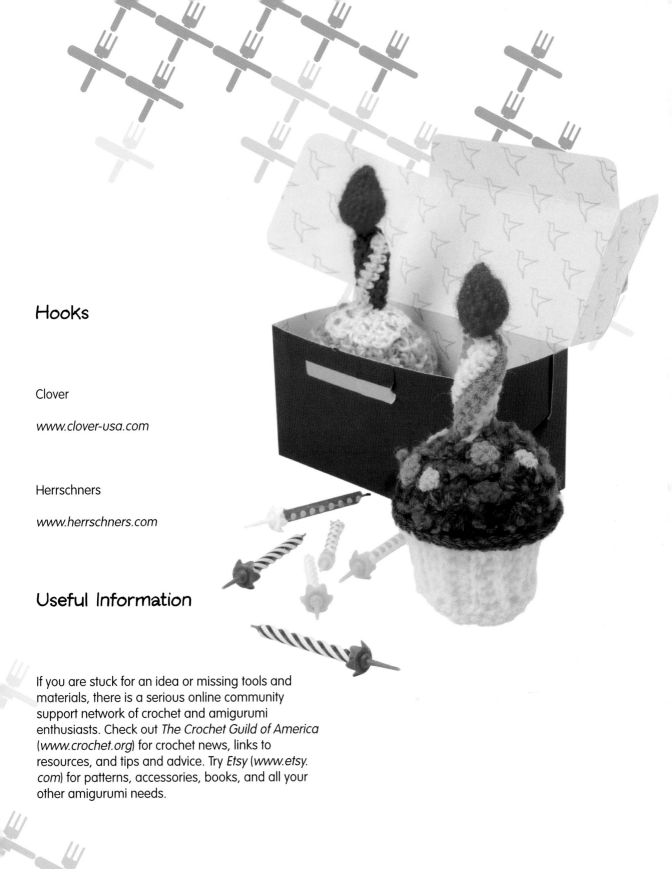

Hooks

Clover

www.clover-usa.com

Herrschners

www.herrschners.com

Useful Information

If you are stuck for an idea or missing tools and materials, there is a serious online community support network of crochet and amigurumi enthusiasts. Check out *The Crochet Guild of America* (*www.crochet.org*) for crochet news, links to resources, and tips and advice. Try *Etsy* (*www.etsy.com*) for patterns, accessories, books, and all your other amigurumi needs.

Index